THE REAL TRUTH ABOUT SUCCESS

WHAT THE TOP 1 PERCENT DO DIFFERENTLY, WHY THEY WON'T TELL YOU, AND HOW YOU CAN DO IT ANYWAY

GARRISON WYNN

New York   Chicago   San Francisco   Lisbon   London
Madrid   Mexico City   Milan   New Delhi   San Juan
Seoul   Singapore   Sydney   Toronto

The *McGraw·Hill* Companies

1 2 3 4 5 6 7 8 9 0   DOC/DOC   0 1 6 5 4 3 2 1 0 9

ISBN   978–0–07–162996–6
MHID   0–07–162996–3

McGraw-Hill books are available at special quantity discounts to use as premiums and sales promotions, or for use in corporate training programs. To contact a representative please e-mail us at bulksales@mcgraw-hill.com.

This book is printed on acid-free paper.

Library of Congress Cataloging-in-Publication Data
Wynn, Garrison.
    The real truth about success : what the top 1 percent do differently, why they won't tell you, and how you can do it anyway / by Garrison Wynn.
        p. cm.
    Includes bibliographical references and index.
    ISBN 0–07–162996–3 (alk. paper)
    1. Success in business. I. Title.
    HF5386.W96 2010
    650.1—dc22   2009016379

To everyone who has come to understand that just being good at what you do is not enough.

Contents

Acknowledgments

I AM DEEPLY INDEBTED TO CERTAIN KEY PLAYERS WHOSE INSIGHT and encouragement were instrumental in bringing about a business book that unconventionally blends straight-shooting truth and slightly twisted humor. At McGraw-Hill, my gratitude goes to Editorial Director Mary Glenn, whose business expertise and guidance made the ride smooth. I will never be able to express my immense gratitude for Mary's patience with me and my staff and the amount of time she spent helping us move through the process of getting this book published and on the shelf. I am indeed grateful to have had the opportunity of working with the best in the business.

Thanks also to Jane Palmieri, whose fine editiorial supervision ensured that my points came across clearly without losing the comedic undergirding that drives those points home.

I express my sincere appreciation for Wendy Keller of Keller Media, who for some time had insisted that the information I present and the humor with which I deliver it had to find its way into a book. Wendy just "got it," and then she went out and pushed it . . . and for her efforts and counsel, I'm grateful.

I would like to give giant thanks to Linda Singerle for making this book a reality. Without her, I'd just be another researcher freaked by my own information. I'm grateful to all the other players who contributed to this book, including Heather Cooper, Jim Eber, Meredith Ellisor, Carrie Rabinowitz, Jonathan Reed, and Jeff Thacker.

David Ratner and Dave Overton of Newman Communications: thanks for the promotional weight you've thrown behind this book.

Thanks also to my wife, Ginger, who made me do this, and to my daughter, Nia.

And finally, I must thank all the interviewees (even those who hung up on me!) for the valuable information they provided; without them, the real truth about success might still be a mystery.

Introduction

My Confession

OVER THE COURSE OF 10 YEARS, I SURVEYED NEARLY 5,000 professionals from more than 20 industries across the nation. I wanted to find common ground among uncommon individuals. I wanted to know what kinds of attributes, skills, and behaviors elevated people to the very top of their field.

My intention was to become an expert on success. What does it take to become the most successful business developer in an industry? What is it about particular managers that make people perk up, perform their best, and smash all existing performance benchmarks when the company's other departments struggle just to meet quotas? Why does one CEO have the undying loyalty of her employees when another causes his people to lose the will to live? I anticipated that the responses would reveal a consensus about pathways to success. I was wrong.

Over and over again, these top performers I interviewed gave the same amazingly boring answers as the mediocre performers. It's one thing to be bored by research; it's really disturbing to be bored by your *own* research. I actually dozed off on one guy who kept using the word "empowered." He was like the Human Sleeping Pill, a superhero fighting to cure insomnia. Had we continued on this path, we would have produced another tiresome and annoying business book with lame, pat answers. I could have called it *Yawn with the Wynn*.

How could the top 1 percent achieve such a tremendous level of success without doing anything different from everyone else? I suspected that the pat answers signaled *too much* consensus. Ever inquisitive, suspicious, and possibly paranoid, I pressed harder, and a handful of professionals divulged strategic information or characteristics they'd leveraged to propel themselves ahead of their peers. My slight personality disorder seemed to have brought the truth to the surface.

I dug in. With humor, approachability, and my own amusing confessions, I plied more top performers, and many of them turned the interview into a confession, admitting the tactics or traits they'd kept well guarded. Before long, I had ample research to blow the proverbial cover off a secret behind success—something distinctive *does* separate top professionals from millions of others. And it is not the double-barreled BS fired into the crowds at motivational seminars. In fact, this get-ahead tactic, although wildly successful, remains relatively unexploited. What's more, this edge exists in all of us, and together we can develop your own distinctive personal advantage—personality disorder not required.

1

Lies about Success—and
Why We Believe Them

Often the truth doesn't sound impressive enough

INTELLIGENCE, EDUCATION, BEST PRACTICES, THE BEST PRODUCTS, great timing—these primary elements take the nation's top business-people to the highest levels of success. At least, that's what we've been led to believe.

These assets certainly don't hurt. But the *most* successful businesspeople get where they are because they have something more: They've got a secret advantage, and they're not afraid to use it.

But they're not willing to share it either. The top 1 percent of successful businesspeople are content to let those myths about success persist. Consciously or unconsciously, actively or passively, they often perpetuate common lies about what it takes to succeed. If they say anything at all, they'll usually attribute their achievements to their greater intelligence, better education, or superior product or service. Others might not step up and boast, but they're not chasing us down the street to enlighten us either. They carefully guard the real truth that some secret personal advantage catapulted them to the top.

Most of the people I've interviewed who are at the top of their game are reluctant to offer up that information, not because they're concerned about competitors gaining a foothold but because they're afraid their secret advantage might not sound impressive enough.

Why acknowledge that landing a position as writer on a top sitcom was more the result of who you know (the producer!) than brilliant scripts and a string of acclaimed successes? Why would you shed light on how lucky you are if you could bask in the fluorescent light of possible greatness? They think, "If people assume I got where I am because I'm the best or the brightest, what's the harm in that?" Having people believe you are amazing is almost as good as actually being amazing. Unfortunately, it also tends to make success seem unattainable by the average person, or even the above-average person.

Yet for many, the secret behind their success packs less of a "wow!" and more of a "how?" as in, "How could it lack this much complexity?" We're left marveling at the simplicity of the plan these top performers chose to implement, not their intellect (*rarely* their intellect). I'm sure a really sweaty guy who happened to be an action taker invented air-conditioning.

Consider, for example, the personal advantages that catapulted these three individuals to the top of their industries:

- An up-and-coming Realtor uses the corporate listings of her husband, a Fortune 500 vice president, to sell million-dollar homes to relocating executives. She becomes a top performer.
- A teen heiress who aspires to model and act pays the paparazzi to follow her and photograph her. The small entourage soon draws a bigger entourage, media attention, and the interest of modeling agents. Contracts soon follow, and she becomes a household name.

- A young mailroom employee cashes in on the power of popularity by talking positively about coworkers behind their backs. When the higher-ups notice how well-liked he is, they decide that someone this popular should be in management. He quickly rises through the ranks and eventually becomes CEO.

These secrets to success are not the kind typically divulged on talk shows or in trade journals. They're just not sexy enough—and in the case of the teen heiress, just a tad disgusting! Even so, the effort of finding and using their personal advantage or distinctive edge produced great results.

Although wildly successful, the use of a personal advantage as a get-ahead tactic remains relatively unexploited by average U.S. businesspeople. And yet top performers on the whole are nothing more than average businesspeople who have discovered their secret advantage and leveraged it to reach new heights.

Hang on. That's a rather unconventional thought! Success can come to the average person who's *not* a standout in terms of skills or knowledge? The prospect seems unfair given the ideas we've been taught. The best man or woman always wins. Right?

Wrong!

Something as simple as a personal edge can boost you to success. And if you don't believe it, that's because you—like so many of us—have been conditioned to believe some lies about success.

The Lies We Believe

We've been fed ideas about what it takes to succeed our entire lives, and we've eaten them up. In many cases, though, we would be better off chewing them up and spitting them out. And that's what we're going to do now with the most common "truths" about success in business:

1. The power of positive thinking propels you to success.
2. To have greater influence, what you have to offer must be bigger, better, more advanced, or greatly enhanced to surpass its competitors.
3. Genius is the foundation of success.

These sound sensible enough. But they're lies. Here's why.

1. The Power of Positive Thinking Propels You to Success

This myth says that, to be successful, it's most important to *believe* you can succeed. That sounds great—except that when you talk to people who are tremendously successful, you learn they did more than just believe: They thought *negatively*. Many professionals have reached the top of their industry because an undercurrent of their own negativity helped them to avoid being blindsided and to prepare for circumstances that could have impeded their progress. They looked ahead to see what problems and obstacles they'd have to kick to the curb. As a result, they didn't hit many roadblocks they hadn't anticipated or planned for.

In fact, a January 2007 study from Jing Zhou, associate professor of management at Rice University's Jesse H. Jones Graduate School of Management, showed that negativity in the workplace can be an effective catalyst for improvement and progress. Zhou suggests that managers should think twice about viewing negativity as an undesirable trait that they should weed out of their workforce. "A sense of dissatisfaction with the status quo, with the way things are right now, can push people to develop ideas and find creative solutions," Zhou explained in an interview.*

*Available at www.explore.rice.edu/explore/NewsBot.asp?MODE=VIEW&ID=9163.

Aha! This explains those cranky people who tend to get under your skin because they actually have good ideas. The study supports the idea that negative thinkers actually fare better than optimists because they've anticipated problems, trends, and instability and are likely to plan to move beyond those fluctuations. Rather than rely on self-assurance to carry them along ("I can do this, I *can* do this, I *can do* this!"), they acquire a little self-insurance ("I can do this because adverse situations A, B, and C can no longer *prevent* me from doing it").

I'm not saying that there's anything wrong with optimism. Honestly, optimists are far more fun to be around. I'm suggesting that the faster track to success is peppered with pessimism. The simple truth that undercuts the power-of-positive-thinking myth is this: When it comes to success, people who see a glass half empty are more likely to fill up the glass than people who see it half full.

2. To Have Greater Influence, What You Have to Offer Must Be Bigger, Better, More Advanced, or Greatly Enhanced to Surpass the Competition

This idea hinges on the flawed premise that the best product always wins. Experience tells a different story: People will choose a mediocre product over a good one, as long as it fills a need.

McDonald's sells the most hamburgers in the world—but are they the *best* hamburgers in the world? (How special *is* that "special sauce," really?) Odds are you can name one or two patty pushers you prefer, and yet McDonald's has owned the top-selling slot for decades.

In this case, mediocrity prevails because the world's largest fast-food franchise fills two great needs: *fast* and *food*. McDonald's is convenient, familiar, and pervasive. We've grown comfortable with it, so it wins our business over better burger joints.

In fact, it's actually quite common for the second- or third-best product to be the top seller because people rarely seek out or choose the best. Instead, they choose what makes them comfortable, whether it's the best or not.

This phenomenon extends beyond products to ideas. Exceptional ideas sometimes fail to take off because they are difficult to understand, while mediocre ideas often rise to the top because they're so clear that everyone can buy into them.

Consider *USA Today*, the largest newspaper in the United States, with a daily circulation of 2.3 million. Written at a sixth-grade comprehension level, the paper built its success on the premise that people want, eagerly accept, and embrace ideas they find easy to digest.

The *New York Times*, on the other hand, is written at a twelfth-grade comprehension level. It sells half as many copies. I once read a *Times* article that used the word *egregious* three times, which I thought was, well, egregious. It made me want to brand *USA Today* as the Fisher-Price newspaper, one that even news newbies could grasp. In fact, I've often thought that if you don't understand *USA Today*, you just might be too dumb to need news.

Few people would argue that *USA Today* is the better or more sophisticated news source. That's not the point. Critics may complain about its "dumbing down" of society with such a simplistic presentation of news. That's not the point either. The sales numbers are the point, and they send a clear message: You'll win greater buy-in if your concept is uncomplicated. If the goal is to get everyone on the same page, shouldn't you at least make that page easier to read?

3. Genius Is the Foundation of Success

This lie about success relies on the misconception that the smartest people are destined to rise to the top: Brilliant person equals brilliant career. But smart is not synonymous with successful.

Lessons at Two Levels

Anyone who has some measure of success as a speaker or presenter knows that many people struggle to see the big picture if it doesn't have detail, while others have difficulty grasping the details without a big picture. That means you need to have both in every situation.

Throughout this book, you'll find some powerful points highlighted in a two-level format. The first-level lesson is a simply stated concept. Its finer applications and drill-down detail are presented in the second-level lesson. Both are important. Without the first lesson, it's easy to lose sight of the second one's value. And without the expanded significance shown in the second lesson, the first-level lesson may appear so simple that it's brushed aside as irrelevant.

The human mind is quirky: It says that if something's too easy, it can't be right; if it's too hard, we give up. With a two-level lesson, the only risk we take is making something too "medium." The result is that this book gives everybody a better shot at understanding the whole message, complete with its most important implications.

The most intelligent, most highly educated person in the company typically is *not* the CEO; this is the little-known guy with his name embroidered on his lab coat. He may be the smartest person in the room, but he has the least amount of influence because people don't know what he's talking about. That's why the smartest people rarely run the company. It's also why if your name is on your shirt, you're probably not the boss.

Many intelligent people lack tolerance for those who don't understand things the way they do. They are seen as poor communicators and have zero influence over an audience. Shooting holes through other people's ideas and insights also undercuts one's influence, so remember that if you criticize others' ideas to advance your own, they will almost never use yours, no matter how good they are. The road to mediocrity is littered with these noninfluential geniuses.

First-Level Lesson

Without clarity, your value doesn't have any impact.

"If you can't tell me in five minutes what's happening in your area of this organization, then you've got zero value." It's a strong statement that generated strong concordance among 479 of the 500 corporate directors and chief executive officers we surveyed. A lack of clarity undercuts your perceived value in an organization.

Lots of people are shocked to learn that clarity, not intelligence, is the biggest determinant of success. People do business with people who are clear. They endorse *ideas* that are clear. If someone communicates clearly and a large percentage of the audience understands her, she has great influence, sometimes regardless of the value of the ideas she's pitching. Her clarity can propel her to a position of success or leadership.

Successful leaders take a lot of criticism for not being intelligent enough. And it's true—often they're not terribly intelligent. But they're perceptive enough to know it, so they listen intently, gather lots of data, and end up with valuable information because they believe they've got something to learn. So if you think your boss is stupid, remember that he's just smart enough to be your boss.

The bottom line is this: Don't let your intelligence prevent you from making sense. It doesn't matter how smart you are if nobody understands what you're saying. If no one appreciates your ingenious idea, it has absolutely no value. Even if you don't consider yourself brilliant, you can still gain more influence than your supersmart counterparts. Remember to strive for clarity, and you just might outsmart the genius.

Second-Level Lesson

If you are clear on a regular basis, people react in a way that establishes you as a preferred source, thus boosting your impact and perceived value.

When you consistently communicate ideas and goals with great clarity, people develop a tendency to come to you for information. They feel good about coming to you because you state ideas in a way they can grasp. Through your clarity, you actually create an emotional reaction in people that makes them want to receive their information from you all the time. You are now seen as The Source, not because of the real value of your information (although it could have great value) but because people have an emotional reaction to the meetings they have with you. They'd rather consult you as the source, even when you're not the *logical* source.

For instance, your department head might have a situation arise that falls outside your area of expertise. Although you are not her optimal source of information for this matter, she so greatly trusts your ability to communicate with clarity that she prefers to come to you for solid information. She'd like to put you in a position to gain the relevant knowledge for this situation and then deliver it to her because she would simply rather get it from you than from anyone else. You actually become the conduit, the preferred way to have anything delivered to her, and you become invaluable to her.

Why We Buy the Lies

Buying into these common lies about success means that many of us unwittingly settle for being average performers, or mild successes at best. The reasoning goes like this: "If I'm not born a genius, then I'd better associate myself with the best product or service out there. Failing that, I'll just have to will myself to succeed."

Of course, not everyone has the IQ of a genius, and a finite number of "best" products or services means a finite number of related jobs or careers. So those lucky enough to be superintelligent or associated with the best products and services have the misguided expectation that success *must* come their way, while all the rest are left to positive-think themselves into achieving. And as most of the U.S. workforce remains preoccupied with these success lies, the more likely path to success—the personal advantage—goes undetected.

So if these lies about success are the very things keeping us from success, why do we believe them and miss our personal advantage? We believe what's *easy* to believe.

Some lies are easy to believe because we've heard them all our lives. There's an environmental factor, a mental conditioning, in play that says, for example, that the best man/woman/product/idea always wins. But there's not a lot of evidence in history to support it.

I once talked with a man who'd been a U.S. tank commander in World War II. "You know how you stop one of those German Tiger tanks?" he quizzed me. "You surround it with 17 Sherman tanks and shoot it until it runs out of gas!" He explained that you couldn't easily destroy a Tiger tank because the technology was far superior; our equipment was no match, one on one. But if you show up in force and just distract it away from the fuel depot it was heading for, well, there's your victory over superior technology.

Another example of mental conditioning comes from nurturing the belief in young people that they can be anything they want to be. Parents, teachers, and society have fed them this idea from birth (that's a topic for a whole other book), and they're convinced that they can be successful if they just *envision* it. It's easy to believe this if you hear it enough.

Some lies are easy to believe because it *feels good* to believe them. We want to think that life is fair, the good guy always wins, and we have enough discernment to choose superior products or solutions over inferior ones. We banish any suspicions that mediocrity can prevail, and we eagerly misplace our belief in some unfailing path of ideal outcomes.

Some lies are easy to believe because it's just simpler to believe them than to question them. Refuting something taxes our minds and requires us to think deeply. Like success myth number two detailed earlier, we often embrace what we can understand quickly. People nowadays *claim* to want more information than ever before in order to make a decision. Yet even with all the information, we still buy into what we can comprehend quickly.

Finally, some lies are easy to believe when they support something that we already believe is true. In other words, if we believe something strongly, we look for reasons that prove our belief is well placed.

If you watch late-night television, you've seen commercials that pump up your belief that you too can drop those unwanted pounds without diets and exercise. Well, you *can*, but that pretty much just leaves disease! And who wants to admit that truth? Put your faith in the magical fat-busting electrical pulses emitted by the BellyMelt VibraBelt—you can wear it while watching late-night TV and eating cold pizza. This is multitasking at its best.

Remember the TV show *Bonanza*? It was the story of a 50-year-old dad and his three 48-year-old sons? We didn't question the plausibility. We suspended any disbelief. Ben Cartwright was such a fair, caring father! And those boys—so loyal! Television is full of examples that underscore our tendency to look for proof that supports the things we choose to believe.

Now before you write off the whole human race as lazy and gullible, understand that some truths are difficult to understand. It's hard to comprehend that being superior to the competition does not entitle us to win. So success myth number two becomes easier to believe because the truth itself is not all that believable. People's choices have less to do with merit than with trust.

The fact is people typically do business with people they trust, people they've got a great relationship with. And when elements like trust and relationship are strong, people become almost blind to differences in quality. It becomes hard for them to discern which choice is truly the best solution. As those lines of distinction begin to blur, people who put stock in the lies about success find themselves at a distinct disadvantage. They need a strategy that will tip the field in their favor.

They need a personal advantage.

Staging the Unfair Fight

As a success seeker, your most effective option is to use your personal advantage to position yourself as a trustworthy, easily understood solution. Whether you seek a job or influence, you want to make sure that everything you do looks like the solution. You want the advantage of people believing in what you do before you do it. Therefore, when you do it, it is received under the good graces of that belief.

I call this *instant image impact*. Your competitors might call it an unfair advantage, but it's exactly what you want in your corner so that you can stage an unfair fight. Because really, the fair fight is overrated. I can lose a fair fight! Give me an unfair fight *and* the upper hand. I'll take those odds any day.

The unfair fight is not a dirty fight; it's just an unfair one in which the opponents are not equally matched. And as we'll see from the successes profiled in the chapters ahead, there's nothing underhanded about getting the upper hand. Some people just have a way of doing things that positions them so well almost before they start that not only can they get better results, but also they're better *perceived* results—thanks to instant image impact.

Much of this impact hinges on appearance. Do you *look* like a solution? Your suit, your haircut, the way you carry yourself—they all go a long way toward recommending you for a particular opportunity. A study once showed that men with long hair couldn't sell anything—except pot. They can sell marijuana like gangbusters; beyond that, they struggle. What does your image tell people you're capable of? Be mindful of it, because that first impression is the filter through which people judge everything else you do.

I know this from a painful experience I had several years ago. I was having lunch with a guy we hoped would join the company. It's our first meeting, and the lobster I order is my first mistake. A close second—the bib I'm wearing to protect my suit. (Never meet a guy in a bib. Bad idea.)

So I've got tools splayed and butter sprayed all over the table. This guy's eating fish with a knife and a fork; I'm cracking shells and spraying lobster shrapnel through the air. Half the table is covered with fallout from me snapping stuff in half.

Despite my mess, the lunch seems to go well, and afterward we stand facing each other alongside the table. We're about three feet apart. I'm talking, and, as I get more animated, I launch this spit mortar—I see it's got a lot of hang time so I wave my hands, trying to get it back or at least redirect it, but it arcs up and all the way over and lands directly on the guy's bottom lip.

It's very difficult to be influential once you've spit on someone's lip. It's pretty much over at that point.

The next day my boss calls up and says, "I heard what happened. You spit in his mouth?" *What?!*

The guy did ultimately come on board, and I worked with him closely, helping him a lot. But four years later, when someone asked him if he remembered Garrison Wynn, he replied, "Oh yeah, the spitter." After all the training and work we'd done, my errant spit was still the filter coloring his perception of my accomplishments.

Leveling the Playing Field

Since then, I've found ways to hone my instant image impact that in no way involve lobster or airborne saliva. And I've spent years discovering what the most successful people in two dozen industries do differently to set themselves apart from their peers.

Some lessons that I've learned from this research are that life isn't fair and rarely are two people equally matched for the situation they face. This means that somebody always has the playing field tilted in his or her favor. If you often find yourself at the lower end of the incline, why not identify and use some personal advantage to level the field? Maybe you won't always have the upper hand, but you will definitely give yourself a better shot at success.

The people profiled in this book didn't do anything illegal or unethical to gain their footing; they were just aware of a unique attribute or resource they could use to set themselves apart. I've designed the rest of this book to help you identify your own distinctive edge that you can use to carve out your path to success. This first step—understanding lies about success—underscores the truth that life just isn't fair and the need to enlist every advantage you can if you want to succeed. Your unfair fight awaits.

2

From Interview to Confession

The truth about lying

OVER THE COURSE OF A DECADE, I ASKED THOUSANDS OF successful people dozens of questions in the hope of discovering truths about success. My staff and I processed nearly 5,000 survey forms, phone interviews, and notes from in-person conversations, looking for patterns and similarities. I attended hundreds of national meetings of various industries honoring top performers and did some one-on-one interrogation. (It's easy to get successful people to talk about their greatness when they've got a big, shiny award in one hand and a cocktail in the other.)

Initially, we thought we had gathered a lot of great information—and it *was* great information! Then, about two years into the project (see sidebar for our methodology) we realized that our fantastic information revealed *way* too much consensus. What we had, I discovered, were not truths about success but truths about lying.

Methods of Surveying

My staff and I spent 10 years discovering what practices and talents the most successful people had in common. We started by considering specific industries and began contacting companies in those industries, asking them to name their most successful employees. We typically sought the companies making the most money, those that were the most financially successful, and then we'd look at the people inside those organizations.

Sometimes we hit a few bumps because we sounded like we were selling something. And some industries were so tough to gain access to that we often found it better to skip around. (The assistant for a top-performing manager at a pet food company was convinced I was a spy for the competition and demanded I admit to espionage. The pet food people are very guarded, apparently. I mean, what's the big secret? You make it stink so dogs love it, and then you say it contains sweet potatoes and sirloin steak to make the humans feel better.)

Company executives would turn us on to success stories at many levels. Some were reasonable: "We're successful because John over here has worked wonders in operations. John created a repeatable process; he made everything so smooth and so effective that life is easy." So we'd talk to John to determine what he does that's different from what other operations people do. Some were downright delusional: A very serious blue-collar supervisor said his secret was that he hired people only from the South because "Yankees think too fast for this job." (Wow, I thought. He managed to put himself down, insult his people, and discriminate against others at the same time. And in just seven words! That's not easy.)

In the end, we took all the recommendations and the people we found and sent all of them our survey. Once the employees returned a completed survey, we'd select respondents to hit with a follow-up phone call with more pointed questions.

In all, we completed about 3,800 phone interviews. In the 10 years it took us to finish, probably only the FBI asked more questions than we did. Come to think of it, we even approached the FBI. What we learned from that experience is very valuable to anyone: *Never call the FBI and say you would like to ask them a few questions!* And that's all I can legally say about that.

We all run into situations in which we do not tell the truth. We want to believe that our integrity is solid regardless of circumstances, but when we get down to the nitty-gritty, we often do what we have to do. We respond and react to the environment or the conditions that are given to us. I've always said that if you put Mother Teresa in a room and starved her, she would kick your ass for a loaf of bread.

So when I asked people about their success, I expected that their truthfulness would vary depending on their current positions or when we surveyed them. Yet whether we were polling the really successful or the phenomenally successful, they all tended to give the *same* kinds of answers—and we didn't believe them. We sensed a double-barreled BS factor. The aroma filling the air was not exactly the sweet smell of success.

Something Stinky This Way Comes

I work hard.
I plan well.
I listen intently.
I gather lots of data.
I build strong relationships.
I present information well.
I have a high level of activity.
My information is superior to my competitors' information.

Repeatedly, our respondents attributed their success to reasons like these—reasons that sounded like standard steps found in many self-help business books. These books can be tremendously helpful—I am, after all, writing one—but I've encountered people who do all these so-called "success basics" without fail and still never stand out in terms of performance. Conversely, I've also talked to exceptionally successful people who do *none* of those things. In fact, I have met people who did the exact opposite of those things and claim that this is what made them successful. I know some really successful business developers who lack time-management skills and who don't plan well; they do something that can only be described as wasting their time with the right people.

In these initial interviews with some highly successful people, the information I got sounded bizarrely average. It seemed like everyone else's information! But these "best of the best" are distinctly *not* everyone else. Millions of people follow these same steps, but they never hit the highest levels of success. There *had* to be a difference, and I was convinced that my respondents had it.

But what was it? The road to success seemed to have a private entrance, and I had found the guard shack, but I was being sent back the way I came with nothing but lame lines that any self-help author could write. What I had learned was this: There's a road I'm not supposed to be on with a funky smell at the end of it. I felt like I was standing in the hall that leads to my teenager's bedroom. There's stuff going on in there that I'm curious about but that she might not want me to discover.

Then I realized that up to that point we'd been looking for *common* threads woven through our success stories. Maybe becoming a phenomenal success had less to do with what you have in common with other reasonably successful people and far more to do with what sets you *apart* from them.

I decided to take a different tack in my interviews to see if my theory had legs. Basically, I became a pleasant but persistent pain in the butt. (Some people I interviewed use stronger words to describe me, but we'll leave it at that.) When I got the standard responses to the "What makes you such a success?" questions, I pushed further. I forced people to look deeper. I made them do more than just answer questions; I got them to confess. I used tactics that would make the CIA proud and Larry King nervous.

"A lot of people work hard, plan well, and listen, but they're not *you*," I pointed out. "They've reached nowhere near your level of success! No offense, but I'm finding it hard to believe that 'empowered brainstorming with laser focus' is *it*! Isn't there something beyond that? Maybe something more specific, tangible, and believable? Can you tell me something that might actually help other people and does not involve a laser?"

We pressed our respondents like this over the phone or in person. And as we steered and personalized the interviews, we could tell that many of our interviewees were caught off guard. That often led to a second answer that, although more personal, still smacked of BS, like this answer I heard from one guy a few years ago: "Well, I guess I owe my success to what my grandfather told me. He said that if you want something badly enough, you can do anything."

"Was your grandfather as successful as you?" I asked.

"Well, not really. We were very poor, actually. He was not a very good provider."

"Hmmm. No offense," I said, "but unless grandpa *wanted* to be a loser, his advice did not help him *or* you. Your grandpauper most likely did not have the ability to help you with the kind of success you've had."

He hung up on me.

I thus learned two valuable lessons about interviewing: (1) The phrase "no offense" is what people say right before they offend you, and (2) never tell people their grandparents are losers. It was a sign of my desperation for the truth.

In the next round of interviews, when I got a second explanation that made as little sense as the first, I'd try again. Particularly in the face-to-face meetings, I'd say, "No offense ..." and then alter my tone of voice to show more kindness with a touch of genuine simulated concern. "No offense, but what you're telling me just couldn't possibly be it. A lot of people do that too, and they're not here getting the top award tonight." Or over the phone I might follow up like this: "Those factors you've mentioned—I bet they do bring you a measure of success, but can you say with confidence that they alone have escalated you to the top-performing slot in your company this year?"

We had hit a nerve. Some people got downright belligerent at the implication that something other than traditional hard work had earned them their place. One very successful writer told me that she was just more deserving of success than others in her industry because of her dedication to high achievement. (She should title her next book Taking the High Road to Arrogance.)

Others simply stuck to their initial pat responses, saying they'd achieved such success solely because they did those expected, average activities far better than anyone else. Does this mean that if you do a lot of stuff that couldn't really make you much better than other people and you do that stuff better than the competition, you're successful? On the one hand, that's from the school of "take care of the little things, and the big things will take care of themselves." Why not work on big things first and handle the little things as they become important?

On the other hand, maybe I had realized something: Sometimes successful people either believe the same lies we've been told or really don't know the truth.

One evening I was dining with a man at an awards banquet held more or less in his honor. He was responsible for about half the company's revenue and good reputation, but he would not or could not provide a credible explanation for his success. Most people in his business were the kind who attend bad networking meetings to try to get business from each other—those events where you meet "hypnotist consultants" and lots of people who have apparently made their own business cards.

But this man did have an advantage, whether or not he would admit it or whether he even knew what his advantage was. I said to him, "A lot of people in the audience tonight have done the things you're telling me, and I'm sure they're wondering, 'How did this guy do it five years in a row? I'm smarter than he is and I have a better business plan! He must have some advantage I don't.'"

He did. And I was just figuring out what it was as others started to reveal some answers that sounded a little less fishy, a little more believable. Take "David," for example.

At 31, David broke into a good-ol'-boy industry that's tough to penetrate and reached heights unprecedented by anyone who isn't, say, double his age. When I first interviewed him, he gave me the same old answers about working hard, being focused, and building relationships. But when I expressed doubt about whether those things were sufficient to put him where he is, he got candid about his appearance.

David's a big guy. And that's an understatement. At six-foot-six and approximately 400 pounds, he stands out in any crowd. So after all the blah-blah about hard work, great focus, and networking skills, he finally got around to explaining in simple terms a key ingredient to his success: "I'm the biggest person that anyone's ever had in their office. I'm unforgettable. Especially in a bright yellow shirt like this one."

David noticed at group gatherings that people followed him like he's the Pied Piper. I told him that I was convinced they were just waiting for an impromptu pizza to arrive. (He looks like he could get Domino's to deliver a pizza to him, personally—not to his house but to wherever he is located.) David countered with his own theory, which you'll hear more about in the next chapter.

The relevant aspect of his story here is that even though he knows he has a distinct advantage and uses it, it was never part of his initial answer to my questions about success. He gave the same responses as my initial interviews, the "consensus" responses. This open, honest, personable guy gave us permission to print anything he told us, and even *he* skirted the question, avoided the whole truth on the first go-round. It seems the truth can make a liar out of anyone.

Coaxing the Truth—from Others *and* Myself

Taking people from interview to confession isn't easy. (If it were, you wouldn't need the information in this book.) In the end, approximately 20 percent of the respondents we spoke to were receptive to the idea that maybe they were doing something unique or different from the masses but didn't know what that was until we prompted them to look a little deeper. In some cases, when pat answers were all they knew, we read to them what their employers or coworkers thought made them stand out, which often triggered a kind of self-discovery. It's like those people who come up with great ideas after they hear the great ideas from someone else and are amazed by their own creativity.

The successful people I spoke to would struggle to dig deep. Some of these top performers seemed to struggle with thinking and just drew from knowledge rather than examining their actions. When we didn't get moving in a productive direction, I would say something like this: "Well, sometimes people have a personal advantage that they use. It may be something innate or an idea they have or a process they use that's different; it may be some information or someone they know."

I soon realized that I was using one of my personal advantages in these interviews: I knew how to use humor and my experiences to disarm people and open them up to revealing more, as if they'd thought of it all on their own. I'd confess that I relied on an entertaining point of view and a funny delivery to set me apart as more effective than my competitors, who presented the very same information—except they often did it in a manner that almost guaranteed that their listeners would quickly stop caring about what they were saying and in some cases actually stop caring about life in general.

I admitted that to offset some of my ADD, I had this practice of taping really big notes to the floor when I was presenting. (I know we're supposed to call it ADHD these days, but the worst thing you can do for people who have a hard time focusing is to indiscriminately add an extra letter to the acronym for their disorder.)

I even reached back to junior high school where, as a quarterback, I was the master of calling audibles with such messed-up cadences that the opposing team would be fooled into jumping offside. I'd instruct my guys to stay put, I'd do my screwy calls, and we'd wait for the opposing team to advance us through penalties. (Well, it works with impatient 13-year-olds.) I know that little ploy could've gotten me in trouble, but unless I was discovered, I was not about to stop using my inside advantage to help me win games. It worked well, and we won consistently, until eighth grade was over. If I had died in the eighth grade, they would have built a statue of me in front of the school. Unfortunately, I lived just long enough to suck! I set the record for throwing the most interceptions in my school's history, with eight in one game. My dad always reminds me it could be a national record. *I would like to take this time out in my book to thank my father for his support and for paying for my therapy!*

My confessions and persistent line of questioning led the wife of one top insurance salesman to confide in me about her husband's unique approach, which triggered a little self-discovery of my own. She said that her husband doesn't come across as particularly sharp or polished or smart. (Ouch! I'd like to see this couple on *Dr. Phil.*) She thought that this put him at a distinct advantage in an industry where slickness, insincerity, and truth-stretching are common and you should be careful about whom you trust.

I interviewed the woman's husband shortly afterward, and I had to agree with her. This guy didn't come across as smart enough to be devious. Almost immediately I was convinced he would not rip me off. I was also convinced that he liked me in the way that only a dumb person can. It's like feeling unconditional love from someone you barely know. It's hard to believe yet entirely real at the same time.

Before long the guy himself admitted to kind of a simpleton approach, which he explained like this: "When I'm presenting ideas, I make things really easy and clear. Then, when talking one-on-one with someone, I get a little lost—on purpose—and they guide me back on track. When they're guiding me to deliver my *own* information, they trust me. I make sure they not only understand what I'm saying but also think they're a little sharper than me. And that allows a lot of the 'big ego' people—people who are in control, who have money—to choose me."

When I heard him explain his process, I realized that you could describe a guy like this in many ways, but dumb is not one of them! It triggered memories from my own experience in the engineering business years ago. In order to talk to organizations about instrumentation, level control, and measurement, I had to learn about their application and their issues. But I found it productive to let people sort of discover how the instrumentation could work for them. I would meet with them and talk about the capabilities of the system I represented, but I would leave out one really big part that I knew they would pick up on. I'd let them explain that to me. And when they were teaching me what they thought my system could do for them, they were actually selling themselves on my product.

Since I'm not an engineer, my success came from the fact that there were holes in my knowledge that I couldn't quite fill. Not telling these engineers their business actually separated me from the competition who tried to be experts. I was highly effective with this approach, but the truth is that I almost *had* to do it that way. My lack of knowledge was my most effective tool.

That's right—it's what I *didn't* know that helped me most. People simply don't like know-it-alls to tell them what they need to do, especially those authorized to pull the financial trigger, those who've got a big position and maybe a big ego to go with it. I was influential at a very high level because I never appeared to know people's business better than they did.

Once the insurance salesman inadvertently helped me stumble across a deeper realization about my personal advantage, I began using it to draw out confessions from other interviewees. It also became a useful tool in my work as a consultant to improve the performance of managers, particularly when paired with a true story I tell that calls to mind the brilliance of the seemingly dumb.

Lost and the Lesson of *Flassie*

I once had to evacuate Houston for a hurricane and then had to "reevacuate"—that's what I call it when everyone rushes back into the place they left in such a hurry. I'm lost on the outskirts of town, so I pull into a gas station where I see this crusty old guy sitting outside. I'm judging him immediately, right? I'm thinking this guy's so old that he looks like he's not going to live through the conversation.

My gas station friend has fishing hooks in his hat, and he's got that faraway look in his eye, like I'm not going to get very good information from the man. I try anyway.

"Excuse me, sir. I'm trying to get back into Houston. Can you help me?"

He says, "What road did you come in on?"

C'mon. You just watched me pull in, didn't you?

I say, "Well, the road *you're* on. There's one road, and you're *on* it. I came here on the road your gas station's on." This guy is not winning any Nobel Prize, I conclude.

He says, "Well, what you want to do is go down the road a piece."

A piece? "A piece of *what*? What does that mean?" I ask.

"You know, some miles."

"One mile? A million miles?" Work with me, gas station man!

"What you do is go down the road a piece. There's going to be like a highway, and there's going to be a hump on this highway; get to the top of that hump, look outcher window and you'll see like a dirt road, a pond, and a trailer park." He pauses. "Don't go in there. Stay on that main road, and take a left where the old schoolhouse used to be."

OK, gas station funnyman. We're going to go over this one more time.

"You're telling me to take a left at a landmark I've never heard of that no longer exists. Is that correct?" Then I snap and use the D word. "Are you just dumb?"

He says, "You know something, son, I ain't the smartest man around these parts. But then again, boy, I ain't lost neither."

I learned a valuable lesson in that exchange: Everybody knows something you don't. The minute you think you know it all, your wisdom vanishes. In that moment when you think you no longer need input from anyone, wisdom leaves you. Your aptitude, your experience, your talent, your skill, and your time on the job—that all stays. Just the wisdom vanishes.

This lesson was as applicable during my encounter with gas station man as it has been in my work as a consultant. When I'm in front of the CEO, the CEO *has* to know more about his organization than I do. The minute I think I know it all, I greatly reduce my power to be effective or influential. I'm pretty sure nothing good comes from telling a CEO that I know more than he does.

Interestingly, the lesson is well known among some of the top performers we interviewed, especially those in leadership positions. We noticed that they were not afraid to admit they didn't know it all. As a result, they knew the value of collecting information from people around them. These leaders might or might not incorporate people's ideas into their decisions, but the information they've gathered allows them to understand where everybody's coming from. They can deliver their decisions in a way that signals a true understanding of what the people around them value. You can deliver decisions in many ways, but you can't be influential unless you know what someone values. So realizing that everybody knows something you don't and then being willing to gather (and maybe even use!) information can position you to succeed in a big way.

Do you remember the TV show *Lassie*? Remember little Timmy? On the show, little Timmy would always be in his house when Lassie would rush in and bark. Timmy would put his hand to his ear and say, "What? What, Lassie? There's a horse with his foot caught in the railroad tracks?" Apparently, Timmy spoke fluent dog.

Remember the TV show *Flipper*? *Flipper* was pretty much just a liquid *Lassie*. Flipper the dolphin could sound off to his human friend who would say, "What? What, Flipper? There's a horse in trouble at the lagoon?" You could put those two shows together and call it *Flassie*.

The point here isn't that I wish I could translate animal talk. (In reality, Dr. Doolittle seemed pretty miserable.) But Lassie and Flipper didn't have to speak a human language or understand the details of their situation to deliver the most important information, which was "Go *now*!" The message of these shows was "trouble's a-brewin', and this animal knows something we don't."

I think most people understand at a basic level that everyone knows something we don't. We just forget that sometimes when it's time to position ourselves to be successful. But people who never forget it, like the insurance salesman I interviewed, have a great chance to stand out above their peers, giving them a distinct advantage.

The Truth about Lying

The insurance salesman's confession, along with my own, helped to elicit "confessions" from a growing number of respondents. Over the final years of interviews, enough people spoke up that my staff and I confirmed the pattern we sensed among the answers:

1. *People who are really successful tend to have some sort of specific advantage.* And some of these advantages you can develop for yourself.
2. *People tend not to admit to an advantage right away.* And some of us appear not to even realize what our advantage is.

Based on some responses I discussed earlier, this second pattern intrigued me most. I began to explore why people gave the traditional answers to our questions and seemed unaware or reluctant to speak about the true sources of their success.

First-Level Lesson

People often do not tell the truth when asked about their success.

If you ask them a simple question about their success and ask no follow-up questions, the chances they won't tell you the truth are great. Success interviews seem to make liars out of the best of us. Two main reasons exist. One is that they don't want you to know the root of their success because they want to appear more valuable than most everyone else. The other is that they think maybe their key to success doesn't sound impressive enough for the results it has garnered. People don't want to admit that the reason everyone loves them is not because of their superior skills, knowledge, or expertise but because they're just good at getting people to drink the love Kool-Aid.

Second-Level Lesson

We often deem irrelevant the smaller things we do repeatedly, but sometimes those seemingly minor behaviors or actions are key to our success.

If someone who's tremendously successful does one particular thing regularly or naturally or maybe even habitually, then that thing—no matter how inconsequential it may seem—should be examined for the part it plays in that person's success.

During our research, we were shocked to hear stuff like this: "Sure, our competitor has got a bunch of friendly people answering the phones, and they're very nice to their customers and all, but there must be something bigger that's causing them to beat us in this market."

Well, if your own people can hardly hide their contempt for customers and meanwhile the competition treats customers with sympathy and respect, I don't think that's irrelevant. In fact, it is hugely relevant. Even the little differences might be the big distinction, the distinguishing factor that gives one person or business a unique advantage over all other competitors.

Some people gave those standard responses because, as we saw in Chapter 1, that's how we're conditioned to think we achieve success. We think we're supposed to talk about it that particular way.

Some of our respondents thought that if others learn that their success is due to something other than hard work, maybe their accomplishments are cheapened. Their success somehow gets sullied. When it comes right down to it, they think their advantage sounds too simple to be respected. It might even invite ridicule!

Some interviewees weren't even aware they were doing something that set them apart until they heard their coworkers' and supervisors' observations. You can't speak capably about something you do if you're not aware you're doing it! I spoke with one jewelry salesperson who sold more items from the jewelry counter than the other 10 salespeople combined. She said, "My coworkers tell me it's because I act like the customer is buying the jewelry for me. They say I get so excited and kind of flirt with male customers and start talking about what I like!" They also said she would always put her hand on the shoulders of these men, which the others seemed to think was inappropriate. "I don't really think that's true," she said. "I'm just good with people." This woman had people telling her exactly why she was successful, and she didn't believe it. I'm not sure if success is as blind as love, but sometimes it definitely needs glasses!

Some didn't realize their advantage until we made them back up and repeat something they rattled off among a bunch of other standard responses. That something was usually done by no one else in that industry. You can't acknowledge something that sets you apart if you think everyone else does it. We talked to a top-performing attorney who said, "I always make sure my clients understand in the beginning that the little knowledge they may already possess of the law will help them a lot. I think that's just common sense to make them comfortable." What?! I think this guy might be the only lawyer on earth ever to say that! When was the last time you heard of a lawyer making clients feel smart before charging them for advice?

Other people were fully aware of their advantage but believed they might jeopardize their success if they divulged the actions they took or the process they used to stand out above their peers and competitors. If shared, maybe their success would become repeatable by many, making them far less valuable to the company, organization, or industry they operate in. Suddenly the Super Successful Guy becomes the Imminently Expendable Guy. No one was all that willing to bring about his or her own devaluation. Successful people naturally protect their success secrets and commonly hold back ideas and tips that will help others. Yet we noticed that low performers seemed more than happy to share the details of their rise to mediocrity!

Ultimately, we found that the people most reluctant to share their advantages were those who had benefited from some family tie or personal relationship that boosted their success factor. If they were positioned to succeed because of a parent or relative or some favoritism, they were the least likely to come forth with it, although a few people were candid or even entertainingly straightforward about it.

One man I interviewed attributed his company's success to the hard work and vision of his father, who had passed away a few years earlier. "My job," he said, "was not to screw it up." He'd maintained the vision his father set, but his father had done all the hard work and built all the goodwill. "I'm his son, I look a bit like him, and I dramatically benefit from that. I don't think I'm anywhere near the good worker he was, and I'm nowhere near the visionary he was. But I didn't screw it up."

This kind of admission also illustrates the big difference between confessing to a personal advantage in business and confessing to other kinds of things like sins or crimes. Outside the context of this book, people generally confess to things because they're guilty of doing something wrong. But almost none of what we uncovered among our respondents was unethical or immoral. Almost none of it would produce any kind of remorse or create some sort of need for cleansing through confession. Using these personal advantages wouldn't make you feel guilty, which is exactly why they're so easy to keep hidden. That's how it was for several top performers I interviewed like David. His appearance is his appearance; it's not unethical or immoral for him to put bright shirts on his large body and let his appearance and intelligence shine equally. Still, he's not likely to readily volunteer that little inside tip because he has no need to "cleanse."

To David and many other respondents, revealing the *exact* truth about their success is something they just normally would not do. The truth hurts. It's hard for someone to admit, "The key to my success is that I have no life and no friends, so all I do is work!" If the ultrasuccessful feel that their advantage is too simple to be respectable, they choose the lie and name several "better" reasons for their success.

For this and all the other reasons we've discussed, most respondents demanded anonymity before they let loose with their lies, let alone the truth. I had one person talk honestly with me and then issue me the dubious warning, "Look, I will sue you into the Stone Age." I'm not sure what that means (he'll sue me to the point where I can no longer have modern appliances?), but he clearly intimated that if certain identifiable information ever got out, I would be in big trouble. In a few cases, we signed confidentiality agreements that prevent us from revealing who some of our respondents are or what industries they're in; we made it clear in those cases that all we wanted were the basics behind their success.

This desire for anonymity is hardly their fault. We humans are always looking for the deeper truth, the more complex explanation of why extraordinary successes happen. The best stories, the most unforgettable movies and television shows are all stories of the hero. They all focus on that special, unbelievably brave soul, right?

The truth is that heroes and cowards feel the same fear; it's the action they take that sets them apart and makes the hero succeed. Heroes generally don't wait to work up some level of bravery before taking action; they take action *while* they're afraid. Sometimes they're not even aware they're acting, so they deem their action to be irrelevant.

And that's what happened here as those top businesspeople guarded their advantages. Only now we know the truth. Think about what we learned from these confessions as we move forward and take an honest look at the natural assets you have, at any reoccurring behaviors and abilities you possess that you might not be aware of, so you can cultivate them into an advantage that boosts your chances of success. Do the introspection and you're well on your way to learning the real truth about your own path to success.

Let's take the next step by considering the innate advantages of size, appearance, image, and personality.

3

The Innate Secret Advantage

I could dunk too if I were seven-foot-two!

Speed, agility, great ball-handling skills, and natural instincts for game pacing and dictating a team's offensive strategies are hallmarks of the NBA's best point guards. Muggsy Bogues had those and more, which led to his selection as a first-round draft pick out of Wake Forest University and a successful 14-season NBA career with the Charlotte Hornets, Washington Bullets, Golden State Warriors, New York Knicks, and Toronto Raptors. Bogues was also—and remains—the shortest NBA player in history.

Short in stature and tall on talent, Bogues faced plenty of skeptics who doubted he could play pro ball in an arena where six-foot-three is considered short. And the skeptics seemed to have a point. If your name is Muggsy and you're five-foot-three, you sound more like a cartoon character than a pro basketball player. But Muggsy's lack of stature actually seemed to help him. Faster and more maneuverable than the hulks, lower to the ground than even the shortest guards he faced, Bogues used his height to his advantage. In other words, he went beyond talent to use what others saw as his apparent disadvantage (his size) and turn it into an innate advantage.

Bogues made an excellent guard, but a center he could never be. That job goes to guys like Yao Ming. Under a 10-foot rim, Ming's standing reach of nine-foot-seven pretty much guarantees him the job, agile or not. I'm surprised a guy that tall can get out of his own way! Yet he has starred at center for the Houston Rockets since 2002 and is a huge celebrity in China. I guess you're destined to play center if you can dunk without your feet ever leaving the floor.

In business, however, innate advantages are subtler than Ming's or Bogues's size and become evident throughout our lives and professional careers. One top performer used his innate advantage of an engaging smile and aura of sincerity underscored by a clean, honest look. As a result, people just naturally wanted to meet him, talk with him, even pay for his lunch. In time, he used the enormous trust people had in him to his advantage, not by being dishonest but by enhancing his ability to sell insurance based on his gift for being Mr. Likable.

In fact, much of our success is based on appearance and personality. They're part of the reason image consulting is a multi-billion-dollar industry. It often takes an image consultant to transform a person's least desirable qualities because, let's face it, we're not all that honest with ourselves about what might need to be fixed. It's like a really wealthy man with horrible teeth. How can he have such devastating dental denial? Does he know he scares kids at the pool?

When it comes to advantages, most of us know the good stuff we got dealt; we just don't use it to get ahead. Yet it doesn't take a consultant to play up any innate advantage you have in appearance, image, or personality. That job's for you! Sometimes it's just a matter of mapping that innate advantage to your goals. This chapter helps you understand the power of your innate advantage.

The Physical Advantage

The world is full of remarkable athletes, but every few years some insanely gifted overachiever commands the spotlight, first by breaking a world record, then smashing it the next time out, and then continuing to obliterate it over and over until we can't help but wonder what freaky genetics are in play there.

Michael Phelps is that athlete. He dominated the 2008 Summer Olympics, winning gold medals in all eight of his events, including some incredible swim-from-behind, win-by-a-hair victories. And winning by a hair is tough in a sport where all competitors shave their body hair before each event!

The man's a machine. He regularly trains six hours a day, six days a week, and he smokes pot! That's impressive! But surely some of the athletes competing at his world-class level must be training and working just as hard. So what's this guy's advantage? What's the deal?

The deal is that the man really *is* a machine ideally constructed to plow through water. Most people have a wingspan that matches their height, but the six-foot-four Phelps has a wingspan of six feet, seven inches. And yet his legs, proportionally, are the size of someone who's just six feet tall. He has hands that have been compared to dinner plates, and he wears size 14 shoes. When you see him on television, you think maybe your TV picture is warped, but that's what he really looks like!

So while an above-average heart and lung capacity power his long-lever arms and dinner-plate hands to create more propulsion than other people his size can muster, his large torso skims boatlike across the surface, followed by short legs that create minimal drag. And then his size 14s shove him forward some more. No doubt about it, Phelps is one maneuverable mutant!

And we're not done. And I'm not talking about his fondness for pot.

Phelps is also double-jointed. Great flexibility in his shoulders, elbows, knees, and ankles gives him fluidity in his range of motion, creating less disruption to his stroke and greater power in his underwater body-flutter thingy. (I'm running short on anatomy adjectives.) In his book *No Limits: The Will to Succeed*, Phelps himself puts it this way: "The flexibility in my ankles means I can whip my feet through the water as if they were fins." That's as impressive as it is disturbing.

If Phelps keeps succeeding, he might even be as impressive as Lance Armstrong, who overcame testicular cancer that, by the time of diagnosis, had spread to his lungs and brain. Some intense chemo, some intense training, and the guy went on to win a few Tour de Frances . . . Tours de France? Whatever. He won seven of them. It's a record, regardless of how you actually say it, and one that is likely never to be equaled.

How did he do it? Is he superhuman? A freak of genetics like Phelps? Partly. Armstrong's heart is one-third more effective than the average man's, and it's thought to be almost a third larger (uncommon but not unprecedented among elite athletes). Some of this is likely the result of triathlon training from his teen years, but there is also some genetic component that allowed him to develop an almost superhuman heart muscle. You can't get that with pull-ups. The Discovery Channel program *The Science of Lance Armstrong* (I have a hard time just going to the gym, and this guy has his own science?) reported that for unknown reasons Armstrong's muscles produce less lactic acid than other people's muscles and that his body eliminates lactic acid more efficiently, leading him to experience less "muscle burn" at the point of peak exertion. He has this great innate ability to push on when most of his competitors are left pushing through the pain.

I don't mean to minimize the grueling training and pure determination of these two amazing athletes by highlighting their innate
advantages. On the contrary! It's important to realize that they willingly trained to improve whatever assets they could. Phelps might
not be able to make his legs any shorter, his wingspan any wider, or
his feet more Phlipperish, but his continuous training can stretch
his endurance, perfect his stroke, and improve his entry and flip-
turn techniques. This guy is just one Darwinian step away from a
gig at Sea World.

Phelps and Armstrong might have abnormal heart and lung
capacities (and, in Phelps's case, abnormal lunch capacity—he puts
down about 10,000 calories a day). But they're not content to leave
that head start unimproved or undeveloped. They train like crazy
to expand what they were naturally given. They recognize and use
their natural physiological endowments. That's exactly what innate
advantages are all about for any top performer. We have all heard
the saying "It's not what you've got but how you use it." The real
truth is that it's a lot about what you've got, and if you don't have a
lot, you might struggle to compete at the highest level.

Upcoming chapters address finding talents, skills, behaviors,
and processes you can use or improve to create your own advantage. But this chapter focuses particularly on some things you may
have been given, some things that are naturally a part of your
makeup or demeanor, that can play to your advantage. We'll start
with appearance and physicality because they are the most easily
identifiable advantages. If you don't have a lot of confidence that
appearance or physicality is your particular advantage, don't be dis-
couraged; there are plenty of other innate advantages we'll get to
shortly.

You might also find it reassuring to know that the most successful people in business are rarely the best looking: Our top 1 percent were pretty average looking, for the most part. Being attractive

can be a great advantage, but good looks are only part of the physical equation. By itself, attractiveness is usually not enough.

Put simply, we must hone our talents, skills, behaviors, and processes to capitalize on our opportunities. But first try to capitalize on the advantages you have been given by nature. You'll still need to maintain and improve them, but you often won't have to look further than the mirror to find them.

Size Does Matter: The Physical Focus

Physical build creates advantages in sports, but do size and physicality create any advantage in the business world? Let's return to the story of David, the big guy we met in Chapter 2.

David was the top performer who made a move from telecommunications into the good-ol'-boy concrete business and ended up dominating the industry very quickly. Concrete is not exactly a walk-in-and-make-a-name-for-yourself business. David, at age 31, quickly carved a niche for himself among businesspeople who typically reward only long-term relationships.

Several things about David enabled him to establish solid working relationships in short order, intelligence and networking ability among them. But it's equally important to know that his frame—at six-foot-six and 400 pounds—makes him a guy you cannot ignore. Especially when he's wearing those bright shirts he's fond of.

You'll remember that after some prodding, David volunteered this information as an advantage: "I'm the biggest person that anyone's ever had in their office. I'm unforgettable. Especially in a bright yellow shirt like this one." To which I replied, "I've got to be honest with you, David. If I were flying over this part of the country in a plane and you were wearing that shirt, I think I could pick you out. I think you're visible from about 15,000 feet!"

David's right. He's the giant in the room. He looks like he should have his own zip code! (I feel comfortable saying that because I've been around him enough to know that he has a sense of humor about his size. Plus I'm pretty sure I can outrun him if he doesn't.)

As he's talking to me, I'm thinking about the people who believe that their size is holding them back. Here's someone who understands that his size is his biggest weapon. He uses his size *not* as a means to an end but as a means to call attention to all the other things he has going for him. He told me that people really are taken by surprise to find a guy who's 400 pounds *and* intelligent. They don't expect him to sound like that. But being big and noticeable and then coming off as smart make him unforgettable. David's success hinges on natural traits or abilities—all of which he works on (even his size is enhanced by those shirts). Take away the size factor, and you have just another hardworking entrepreneur.

David's success equation: 1 smart salesperson + 1 good networker + (6'6" + 400 lbs) = success

OK, so that's not a formula that many people can duplicate. Few people are six-foot-six *and* 400 pounds *and* smart *and* personable, but my point is that you cannot limit yourself to simple measures of beauty: You might have an important physical trait that helps you stand out or helps draw attention to you.

David of the day-glo shirts believes his size has some sort of magnetic draw in a crowd. He'd be talking to people at a trade show, and after the conversation he would head across the room for a drink and turn to notice people following him like he's the Pied Piper. He believes part of the draw stems from prehistoric instincts—like in the days of the caveman, when the clan just stuck by the biggest guy. The biggest guy was in charge; he was good for protection and preservation of the species.

David may be onto something. And I propose that his modern-day appeal is that he's not only big but people know he's intelligent too. We humans like to put our trust in those two things. We believe in Giant Smart Guy. We see Giant Smart Guy, and we want this guy on our team. He can protect us *and* enlighten us. He is a brains and brawn combo! That's doubly advantageous. If you seek leadership and a buffet, following the Giant Smart Guy is your best bet.

The idea of size as an advantage plays to a theme that surfaces again and again in this book: For the position you're trying to obtain or the problem you hope to solve, *do you look like the solution?*

For example, in leadership positions, height is an advantage. Very few company CEOs are five-foot-three. The most powerful world leaders typically are tall (and the short ones seem pretty cranky). People portray Napoleon as short, but that's a misconception. At a little over five-foot-six, he was an inch taller than average in his day. His comparative stature today would be equivalent to a height of six feet. (His reported height of five-foot-two in French feet, or *pieds de roi*, was not commonly converted to the English measurement. Plus, he was often painted while posing near over-sized furniture and the unusually tall Imperial Guard.)

I'm not saying that you have to be seven feet tall or 400 pounds to succeed. But if you don't look like the solution, you'll need to be exceptional in other ways. Size and stature are simply baseline physical characteristics that can give you an immediate competitive edge in the right situation. Then you can use that advantage to open the door for all the other skills and talents you can bring to a certain position.

I once interviewed the top salesperson at the largest car dealership in the country. Before the interview, I had no idea what he looked like, only that he was great at what he did. As I waited to meet him, I looked up to see a young African-American man rolling his wheelchair toward me. I have to be honest: I wanted to buy *my* next car from him, and he was still about 20 yards away from our first encounter. I asked him if he felt people pitied him and if that helped him sell.

"Only when I drop my notepad on the ground and they lean over quickly to pick it up for me," he said.

"How often do you drop it?"

"Well, only when I have to!"

Like David, this salesman is not bothered by the fact that something about his appearance plays to his advantage. It draws potential customers in, where he can immediately use his other abilities to make them more comfortable and trust him. Would he like to walk? I'm pretty sure anyone in a wheelchair would like to walk. But there's a lesson here for all of us: If there's some physical aspect about us that we can't change, why should we shy away from it? Believe in it and use it!

Being Good-Looking Is Good

Humans are hypocrites! We want to believe that candidates for a position should be evaluated on the basis of experience and qualifications. Yet, when job applicants interview, we often show a bias toward good-looking candidates. Our bias minimizes any lack of experience they might have and smoothes over gaps in their qualifications. ABCNews's *20/20* examined this issue in a special called "The Ugly Truth." The producers sent two pairs of actors—male and female—with equal qualifications for job interviews. When faced with nothing more than physical difference, the interviewers were not only nicer to the attractive candidates but also valued them more. The fact that most top performers in any industry (other than entertainment and modeling) do not have movie-star looks does not stop people from preferring the hot and handsome!

So, we like to think we live in a meritocracy, but biases are always prevalent when it comes to good looks or any unique physical characteristics that draw people in quickly. This counts when you're not in the room as well. Does your Web site still have the picture of your employees lined up in rows in front of the building, some kneeling, some standing, some appearing constipated? If your site has bad graphics, especially of your people, it doesn't matter how good your *company* is, how much good information you have, or what services you provide. Sure, some customers *might* stick around your site long enough to read all you're capable of and how you've been in business for 150 years. But no one ever says, "Hey, this is a horrible site! Let's contact these people and see if they can help us." If customers don't like the interface, they'll click away, maybe to the clean graphics and good-looking guys on the competition's site. They might even go so far as to contact your better-looking competitors to ask if they offer the services you described on *your* site!

The truth is that bad Web sites sell the competition. It's like eating bad food; it just makes you hungry for a good meal. That's how hugely important it is for people to see you in your best light.

That's why some companies still hire for looks—a throwback to the early days of airline travel, when flight attendants were young, attractive women who were called stewardesses and had certain age and weight limits. Several decades later, our "enlightened" culture has sophisticated companies that have used cutting-edge marketing and sales data, chewed over the numbers, and decided that people respond the strongest to 25-year-old attractive blondes. So that's their sales force, and they expect the looks to work to their advantage to close the sale.

This is especially prevalent in the pharmaceutical industry. In the office setting, physicians are generally pressed for time. They don't drop patient care and research for just anything—except maybe for pretty blonde women bearing gifts. "If she's got free samples, she's 25, and she's good-looking, I will see her." That's what pharmaceutical sales divisions often bet on.

News programs are the same way. News anchors are often beauty-pageant competitive, at least on TV. That's the type producers are looking for to connect with their audience and draw people in. It's how people like their news delivered. The key is to deliver bad news with good-looking people. Good news may not sell, but good-looking people can keep us glued to the TV with the latest bad news followed by a commercial for antacids. Need a few regular, average folks for balance? Let them do the weather.

Sure, in some cases, being really good-looking is a disadvantage. Good-looking women seem to be able to sell to women, but I've noticed that salesmen who look like movie stars don't sell well to men. They sell well to women. They struggle in sales positions where most of their prospects are men. Men don't like to write checks to guys who they sense are proof that our baldness and bellies do not go unnoticed.

Being attractive is usually a plus, so if you've got this innate advantage, use it. Yet most people aren't willing to do it. They either overdo it (the girl behind the hotel front desk apparently enamored with her own good looks) or "underdo" it (the handsome bank employee who has made that life-changing decision to keep the unibrow regardless of the fact he scares children).

The lesson here is that the people who are gateways to success are likely to be making unfair assessments based on outward appearances. Your job is to present yourself as attractively as you can. You can't consider it unfair that someone is attractive; you can consider it unfair if that person uses it as a weapon. If you are unusually good-looking, there's no need to play that down out of some sense of fairness unless you suspect your looks are hurting your credibility in some way.

First-Level Lesson

Don't dismiss how you're designed.

Lots of people ignore their own innate advantage because they can't see how it delivers any professional edge. It's a mistake to downplay or shrug off something about your appearance or physical makeup because it doesn't directly indicate professionalism or qualifications for the opportunity at hand. Maybe your smokin' looks or your instinct for dressing well don't indicate how qualified you are for the job you want, but they sure make you look like someone people will open doors for. So when the door does open on account of a physical advantage, you just need to make sure all your other excellent qualities rush right through it.

Steer clear of the idea that the only innate advantages that count are related to IQ or mental quickness or a head for numbers or other "worthy" professional qualities. An innate advantage is anything that you possess naturally that can help you succeed. That's a very large category, encompassing everything from being a naturally good listener to being the person in your neighborhood who all the dogs seem to like. (Having bacon in your pocket does not count!) Listening can help with every relationship you have and turn you into a trust-building machine. Being popular with dogs could also do the same—we tend to trust the people our dogs love and distrust the ones who make our canines growl.

The myth is that only the innate qualities involving esteemed abilities in the professional world are worthy of our attention. The real truth is that understanding what your innate advantage really is, honing it, and having a plan to use it effectively is more important than the type of innate ability you possess.

Inequality: To Your Advantage?

Size, appearance, and physical makeup count for a lot, but they're not everything. Being a tall blonde does not make you a news anchor; height does not automatically earn you a leadership position or a job as starting center in the NBA. These advantages help but, as we saw with Phelps and Armstrong, they're no guarantee, nor are they the *only* advantages.

A lot of football players are fast and big, but how long can they last if they're repeatedly colliding with or trampled by 300-pound guys? In football, durability is often the differentiator beyond size. Brett Favre had talent—and an inability to say good-bye—but his stature was greatly enhanced by the fact that he was never injured (enough) to miss a start. Remember Bo Jackson? He was supposed to be the second coming in football *and* baseball but never played much outside college because of injuries. Countless others you never heard of failed to make it out of college or even high school. Running back Jimmy "Glass Knee" Nelson never had a chance!

Let's get real. Some people are just hard to kill or are immune to the problems plaguing the general public. When the bubonic plague swept through Europe in the Middle Ages, one-third of the population died. But two-thirds didn't. Many people exposed to the highly contagious disease didn't even get sick. How can some people literally eat garbage out of the dumpster and be okay while others die because they are allergic to shrimp?

So there are advantages and disadvantages to be found in inequality. One thing's for sure: All human beings are not created equal. We should have equal rights, but we're not the same physically, mentally, emotionally, or spiritually. We're not born into the same communities, families, or money. A lot of people seem to be created a lot alike, but they're not equal.

If you're not built to be an athlete, give it up. Right now, no matter how much I want to win a gold medal for swimming (or even compete on a high level), I have to face the fact that unless I'm Dara Torres or joining some senior pool circuit in Florida, I'm old. And I don't swim well. I just s l o w w w l y   d r o w w w n   across the pool. There's no medal for that. (What you get for that is a hospital wristband.) Here is a headline you will never see: *Old Slow Guy Wins Gold!*

An advantage must consist of more than something you're trying to do; it's something you can deploy easily and use repeatedly to keep up and ahead. It's important to recognize whether your advantage is sustainable. If it's not, it's not much of an advantage. Learn what limitations you might have that make you unsuitable for a particular opportunity or position.

Second-Level Lesson

Know what you're not designed for.

Positive thinking tells us that, even though we have failed time and time again, we must keep pushing forward regardless of disappointing results. However, it is possible that we just naturally physically or emotionally *stink!* We might have to face the fact that we lack the key trait or innate ability to be good at something. Whatever other people often tell you that you do well is where your abilities lie. If you tell your spouse, "Honey, I'm going roller skating" and your spouse replies, "Okay, but *please be* careful," it means you're not a skilled skater. If you don't have very good balance, you will never race with Lance Armstrong in the Tour de France or Tours de . . . whatever . . . you're not going to excel at anything that requires balance in France (or anywhere else, for that matter). It's hard to focus on your distinct advantages if you are working hard on the ones you don't have.

The reason these sports analogies are useful—and the reason top athletes are so successful on the speaker's circuit—is that their successes are familiar and their innate advantages are easier to see. How long do you think Bobby Knight, the famously abrasive, hotheaded, and hugely successful college basketball coach, would survive in an office environment? He'd be dead in a ditch with knives in his back. But I'd be willing to bet he knows this too. He seems to have leveraged his advantages quite well in his career.

Can't detach from a situation? Don't be a doctor. Doctors need some bedside manner, but they must be emotionally cold and distant when considering the symptoms and making a diagnosis. Consider the alternative: a doctor who's an emotional wreck, crying and freaking out every time he or she delivers bad news. It's difficult to be a heart surgeon if you keep sobbing while explaining how the surgery will go.

It's the same in business: Know the limitations of your advantages—know where you are unequal and when you are in an unfair fight. Don't like people much? Hate being responsible for their mistakes? Being a supervisor will be hard for you. If you don't like people (and you know who you are), stop trying to manage them. If all your employees hate you, you're not a leader! Leave that job to someone who can handle people and shoulder blame. You are not that person's equal in this job. But you can be sure that there are some aspects of you that the other person cannot equal that will help you lead elsewhere.

It Takes All Kinds—What Kind Are You?

It's a big mistake to *wish* that people were all born equal or to try to turn people into equals. Again, I'm not talking about equal rights; I'm pointing out what a mistake it is to pretend that we are all the same. I often speak to managers who want to increase their department's productivity. Many of them will say, "I'd like a perfect, well-rounded team that gets along well." *Why?!* If you've got a bunch of people with the same disposition, the same thought processes, the same information, that's not a team; that's one person cloned several times over.

Here's a better team:

- *The vision person:* "I see it. I see *everything.* I see the future."
- *The butt kisser:* "I see whatever you see, and it looks fantastic."
- *The negative thinker:* "I see it, and I see every problem we'll have along the way."
- *The lazy one:* "I see it, and here's the easiest way to do it."

This well-rounded team knows where it's going, supports one another, anticipates and plans for the obstacles, and does so in a time-saving, resource-conserving manner. Team members might not love one another every day—and having butt-kissing guy and negative person carpooling could get weird—but it will work far better than a team of people who have the same thought processes and hold the same beliefs.

The true strength of a team is based on the fact that people play different positions. The strongest organizations have strong people with different talents coming together to tackle problems and create solutions. Disagreement is more than just a platform for a bad day; it is often the foundation of consensus. Disagreement comes from the people who see things differently. As insanely obvious as that sounds, it is the key to good judgment.

The idea that we all have to be a certain way or equally gifted or equipped is ridiculous. Certain jobs or roles require a dominant set of skills or attitudes balanced by almost a complete absence of another set. My lack of skill as an accountant allows me to ask questions I wouldn't if I knew more. I am ignorant enough to know I need the counsel of those who specialize in accounting and confident enough to seek it out and then question anything I don't understand. In the end, my organization's books are better.

The world has to be made up of all types to function. So what type are you? Aside from any physical advantages that might set you apart, what attributes or behaviors come naturally to you? Maybe it's a certain aspect of your personality that gives you an advantage you can play up.

For example, if everyone trusts you and likes you, you need to be in a position where that helps you to succeed. Being the friendliest guy on the garbage truck means very little. But start promoting sanitation services, and you just might get somewhere. Can you become the face of sanitation services and trade on the fact that the people who can advance you know and like you? Now you've got something. Being the "face of garbage" in your community might not be everyone's dream, but it shows that even if it's your job to be dirty, you still can clean up in your industry.

If you're a perpetual cheerleader—constantly building people up and encouraging them—you like to motivate people. You've got a leadership quality that's really hard to teach, so you need to be in a position where you're helping to move people forward. But if you're not in a leadership position, you'll just be that annoying employee who has apparently consumed so much corporate Kool-Aid that no one wants to go to lunch with you.

In Chapter 2, we learned about the insurance professional who doesn't come across as savvy enough to get the best of anyone. Rather than working hard to be slick and sophisticated, he decided that being naturally genuine and uncomplicated could set him apart. He might not come across as intelligent, but he's being unbelievably smart: He understands exactly how to read people and come across. He knows when it's time to talk business and when it's not. He earned a great deal of trust among his prospective customers and respect among his peers. And he earned a great deal of money too. I once heard someone use the term "dumb money." A bitter, brilliant, broke person probably coined that phrase.

I once had a girlfriend who had this magnetic quality about her that she exploited. She looked like a cross between Audrey Hepburn and Demi Moore (an immense improvement on my college girlfriend who looked like a cross between Katherine Hepburn and Michael Moore). She had this way of touching people when they talked that was not intrusive, just very natural. It was a subtle but powerful way of conveying warmth, approachability, and (benign or serious) flirtatiousness in one gesture! She took a job selling makeup in a mall, and in three weeks she ranked among the top-selling representatives in the country. Her allure was so strong that without any dirty tricks—just her unfair advantage—she sucked customers away from other counter workers who threatened to quit. She knew her type: Her innate advantage rested in that ability to easily draw people to her. Even 40-year-old men began buying makeup from her (men who couldn't tell makeup from shoe polish). I thought she was my soul mate, but after a while I realized that if she really *was* my soul mate, there must be something horribly wrong with my soul.

Sometimes your advantage is not something different but something that makes you so much like other people in some way that they immediately identify and empathize with you. Oprah Winfrey is a great example of this kind of innate advantage.

Oprah is just more of what her audience likes and relates to. She struggles with her weight, opens up about difficult childhood issues, talks publicly about her relationships, and more. But she was told early in her career by a news director that she needed a makeover if she hoped to remain competitive delivering the news; she did not look the part. But that was the point: She looked like *all* the parts, and she was determined to use that to her advantage. Today, she's got the empire to exploit her advantage with her audience, who is made up of people a lot like her. Winfrey is very talented, but she exploits an exceptional ability to convey sympathy or empathy through her own stories and her guests'. Even I have to admit that when I watch her show, just for a few minutes, I feel she is talking to me—even when the topic is temporary water weight gain.

Case Study: From Receptionist to CEO

One CEO's story from my research demonstrates an ideal blend of innate advantages such as drive and perceptiveness with other advantages that she developed (ones we'll explore in later chapters).

Mary was first hired as a receptionist for a nonprofit professional organization in the 1970s—a time when receptionists had big hairdos and little opportunity. Seven months later, when the CEO's assistant gave notice, Mary got the position and decided to start her lessons in executive management. She noticed how her boss delayed his commute home until traffic to the suburbs thinned out.

Mary's innate desire to learn and her natural common sense told her not to squander the opportunity in front of her (access to the big guy!). What better mentor could she ask for? If you're going to pick a mentor, why not choose someone who can fire anybody who gets in your way? Although she lived nearby, she stayed late too.

"I would hang out in his office, and he would tell me stories," she said. "He would talk about what it was like to be working at the legislature doing lobbying, which was a big component of the role. And he would tell me about the history of the organization and about politics. I would sit for anywhere from half an hour to an hour and a half and just listen to him tell me about what the environment was like.

"If he was there and willing to talk to me, I was going to take advantage! I got exposed to all kinds of information and perspectives that I could never have gotten otherwise, with other people around. It also gave me a lot of insight into how he thought about things, which made me really useful to him and to the organization. . . . I could help people figure out how to take an idea or problem to him or how to resolve an issue because I knew *him*. It was kind of like being Radar to [*M*A*S*H*'s] Colonel Potter."

Too often, people like Mary—natural leaders trapped in entry-level jobs—don't want to work the extra six hours a week it would take to learn, even if it means earning more. (Great ability without ambition may mean you're a talented loser.) And here's Mary, on a secretary's salary, jumping at the chance to spend an extra three to six hours a week at work. She couldn't have anticipated the ultimate payoff, which was still about 16 years off. She did what she did because her innate curiosity prompted her to learn more and her innate drive pushed her to be as useful and valuable to the organization as she could.

Over the next decade, Mary took on additional roles in the organization with increasing levels of responsibility, always mindful of what aspects of the business operation she needed to learn. Somewhere around her twelfth year there, she became the organization's deputy director and also took responsibility for its continuing education program (a role for which she was perfectly suited, given her dedication to her own continuing education).

"That role allowed me to learn the one really big component of the operation that I didn't have any background in," Mary said. "It was a piece of the organization that really could give me the big picture. Even though I thought the job would be awfully dry, I knew it would position me as a potential candidate down the road."

Sure enough, five years later, the CEO announced his retirement and a nationwide search for his replacement began. An outside consulting group and a committee consisting of members of the statewide organization considered 193 candidates. Mary won the job—all because she used every advantage she had to take the right steps at the right time with the right person.

Mary's story is all the more amazing when you consider the office culture that surrounded her journey. As a fresh college grad in the mid–1970s, Mary knew that being a woman (let alone a woman who had been a lowly receptionist) in a male-dominated profession typically meant you were locked into a set of expectations and locked out of the executive level. So, in addition to her desire to learn as much as she could, she had an innate ability to withstand some inappropriate comments or off-color "guy talk" and turn down the occasional advance without making the boys who could hurt her advancement feel bad. Telling someone that he's the last person on earth you'd ever date without making him feel bad takes true talent.

The real truth is that putting up with bad behavior unless that bad behavior becomes toxic is typically more effective in business than standing your ground. I might catch a lot of flak for that last sentence, but people who refuse to tolerate high degrees of unacceptable corporate behavior are not the ones with the most influence and opportunity (although their story just might get made into a TV movie). Tolerance tends to be more profitable. And while I know people can learn to do this, I consider this an innate ability.

Here's Mary's approach, as she explains it:

"I came into the organization when it was male dominated, and I was often the only female in the group, whatever that group happened to be. Although I was typically doing secretarial or administrative things, I got to hang out with the guys. And I did it always recognizing that I had to be careful about *how* I hung out. I knew that at any time if I were inappropriate—if I came across as some stereotypical 'dumb blonde' . . . I had to be credible as a person, and I put a lot of energy into understanding what the guys were talking about, making sure I could hold my own in a conversation.

"I really worked well in that kind of environment. I get it about how they function and how they like to work. . . . They didn't want to have to change who they were; they wanted to be comfortable.

And I had everything to do with whether it was comfortable when I was around. I was attuned to that. . . . I was aware that you don't have to be a battle-ax, and you don't have to be the ditzy blonde. You can be smart and present yourself well and still make work comfortable and fun [regardless of gender]."

Mary knew that the other women in the organization and the wives of the guys she worked with could easily resent her: "I understood that dynamic was in play." But she emphasized that the advantage, if you examine it, isn't really about gender. A man who refused to play along would have it just as bad, if not worse. "If you clear all the gender stuff out of the way and look at the plain version of it, [my innate advantage] was about recognizing the people you're working with and adapting appropriately."

Mary had a high threshold for tolerating the politically incorrect long before political correctness took hold. (In the 1970s, "politically correct" meant you didn't mention that the country recently fired the president for burglary.) But she also relied heavily on advantages like self-knowledge (knowing what you're about and staying true to that) and the desire for self-improvement (recognizing those opportunities for learning and advancement as they present themselves). Mary's killer combination of knowledge-based and innate advantages was her key.

Mary rose to a leadership position in a male-dominated industry, and yet she doesn't attribute her success to anything that has to do with her being a woman and how she dealt with men. In fact, she might balk at my reference to her innate ability to tolerate more guy talk than her peers. She might argue that her innate advantage was her ability to read her audience and adapt without compromising her identity.

The real truth is that we're both right: In business you have to be able to weather the storm *and* look pretty damn good in a raincoat.

Turning Disadvantage to Advantage

Some of the examples in this chapter should have struck a chord with you or at least prompted you to examine the obvious or hidden innate advantages in you. But if you're searching and all the innateness you find appears to be disadvantages—well, don't worry. We found that some of the most successful people we interviewed were manic and scattered. A few were borderline insane. So don't let the fact that you feel like a nutty mess stop you from taking a shot at greatness. That nuttiness might be your edge!

The next step then is to discover ways you can create your own advantage out of some things that appear to be disadvantages.

4

Why Would Anybody Want to Be in a Fair Fight?

Create your own advantage

IF YOU HAVE TROUBLE DISCOVERING AN INNATE ADVANTAGE — OR if what you find doesn't seem advantageous enough — you *create* an advantage. The top 1 percent we surveyed and studied did not always have size, beauty, or remarkable demeanors (some were downright obnoxious and a bit hard on the eye), but they all had advantages they used to help them be successful. These advantages were often not innate but things a lot of people *might* have. The top performers just identified the potential advantages and, if they did not have what they needed to create them, went out and got it.

Creating an advantage is not easy, especially if you have no talent, but it is always possible. Just think about people you've worked with over the years: unimpressive, untalented, and eventually in charge. As you read this chapter, look around you. What does success look like? What do those successful people have that you don't (other than success, obviously)? Chances are they have more than innate advantages. Try to discover some learnable behaviors or positioning strategies that you could duplicate. Is there an education level that can't be maneuvered around? Is there training or certification needed?

As you look around, remember that it's important to know the business culture you're operating in. You must see business for what it really is: a place where fairness falters, where even the seemingly undeserving win. The terms "fair fight" and "level playing field" have little business in the business world. The bottom line in the real business world is that fairness rarely raises its ugly head. A fair fight means you are unprepared. Heck, I could lose a fair fight. I personally like my fights lopsided in my favor and my opponents minimally skilled and easily defeated. Let's be really honest: You want a fair fight only if you believe that equality is more important than personal success or if you are bored with how easily you've been winning your fights. When I first started to hear the advantages of the most successful, it did not seem right that they were successful regardless of talent, skill, or education. But I realized that the people who are willing to overcome everything in their path (like a giant lack of talent) because of their desire for their goal were as deserving as anyone else.

Viewing business this way requires a willingness to step away from traditional norms of fairness—to understand that "unfair" fighting does not mean unscrupulous or dishonorable. It means thinking critically about some business practice, personality trait, or personal strategy and then methodically employing it to your advantage so you stand out from others and win. Creating a phony Facebook account for a person who is competing with you for a promotion that clearly states his dedication to Hitler is definitely unscrupulous. However, making sure you discuss your love of the History Channel in the interview with your Nazi-crazed future boss is not. You knew what he valued and got excited about his favorite subject. And you used your thought-to-be-useless knowledge of World War II to get the promotion.

First-Level Lesson

A fair fight is for the unprepared.

Getting ready for an unfair fight does not mean that you'll be doing something dishonest or unscrupulous. It means looking for the advantages you have and being willing to use them to win. Plain and simple, life is not fair. The same goes for the business world. We need every advantage we can get to guarantee success. Being prepared is the basic ingredient to improving your chance of success in any endeavor.

Business Culture: Where Fair Play Fails

To create a personal advantage, you have to see the *real* business world, not the *ideal* one. This requires unconventional thinking and planning and a clear understanding of the most challenging aspects of business culture today. In the real business world, people who are not very good at what they do get achievement awards, and mediocrity becomes the new "innovative." You'll need more than talent, skill, and your disdain for mankind to compete.

Businesses are full of difficult people, and "difficult" can take many shapes: the vindictive, the deluded and jaded, the egomaniacal, the eternally pessimistic, the mentally ill. Corporations are also populated with people who aren't particularly smart but have some other qualities about them that they use to further their careers while frustrating the people around them. Maybe they have a personality that wins them the popular vote at the expense of the better choice. Some people are so likable that we don't care that they can't really do anything (and that's a true innate advantage). And then we have those people who grumble at the prospect of innovation and impede opportunities for progress. Working alongside folks like this presents special challenges, especially when their shortcomings seem so obvious. Some people are stupid, and some people are pro-jectile stupid—this means that their stupidity actually reaches out and makes those around them unintelligent.

As we saw in Chapter 3, people often get selected to fill positions or provide services based on looks or likability instead of qual-ifications. It seems that the connection between success and intelligence has been grossly exaggerated. These people get pro-moted even though they are *not* the best fit for the position. They receive awards because they're popular and they happened to do a pretty good job or the right job (but certainly not the *best* job). I know a guy who was named employee of the month six times in a row because he spoke Chinese and translated for the management team. They did all the work. He just spoke the language.

Think about this in terms of politics: Candidates who can't speak glibly or very clearly and who look awkward on camera never win a presidential election. This says a lot about what most people subconsciously deem as "qualifications":

- Photogenic? Check.
- Confident-looking? Check.
- Able to squeeze grand ideas into simple sound bites? Check.
- Does not speak in compound sentences? Check.
- Unusually large head? Check.
- Elected!

It is the same in the business realm—with hiring processes, promotions, recognition, and more. Maybe you don't consider your-self very political, and that's okay. But if you're in a political (read *business*) environment and refuse to play politics, you're going to lose the unfair fight to someone who does. You are essentially saying, "I'll roll the dice and take my chances." And there's always a chance you'll roll snake eyes.

So, stop using words like fairness and start creating your own advantage by looking at what's considered important in your "political" environment: What is the impression you make on people? How do you come across? Do you seem like a fit for the job you have? If you're a cranky, judgmental person who tends to see something wrong with everyone and everything, customer service is not in your future. But you *are* a natural-born safety inspector. The truth is if you're a smiling, trusting, happy-go-lucky safety inspector, something is going to blow up.

The Right Person for the Role

Beyond any innate advantages, how can you make an impression with the other skills and abilities you possess? If you cannot walk away from a problem without resolving it, even if it takes you *days*, consider the information technology field—you're destined to debug. Directed the right way, the same quality that drives your friends batty— "I don't care if it takes six hours! We're not leaving this table until that waiter splits that $15 calamari charge across *all* our receipts. No way that squid y'all ate lands on my Visa!"—might be your ticket to success. Don't ignore your (ahem!) gift. Embrace it. Channel it.

Have you worked hard at something every day for the past five years without getting any better at it? Stop! Give it up! Do something else. My father thought he was a fix-it guy. What we learned was that if Dad is working on something, we are definitely getting a new one. Dad stinks as a fix-it guy. My shop teacher had a finger missing on his right hand. He knew how to work the power tools;

he just wasn't very good at it. At the beginning of each semester, he'd hold up his hand missing a finger and say, "Let's talk about safety." No way I'm learning safety from you! The lesson: You can't lead by example if you're a bad example. You have no influence.

From our surveys, we learned that the top 1 percent understand this secret: Do very little of what you do badly and a lot of what you do well. If you don't do something well, stop doing it in front of the people you're trying to influence. It's like people who don't know how to surf who go to California once a year, rent a surfboard, and go for it. It looks like a strange mix of danger and sadness. In reality, it's just controlled drowning.

The overriding concept is that you're most competitive when you get better at what you already do well. It's an important conclusion drawn from a Gallup study of 80,000 managers and 1 million employees. The study results, presented in the book *First, Break All the Rules* by Marcus Buckingham and Curt Coffman, aligned tightly with responses that showed up consistently in our interviews with the top 1 percent: Successful people do very little of what they do badly and a lot of what they do well.

As simple as that sounds, people forget that. I've seen lots of strugglers over the years—people who do all the right things and still don't succeed. They suck at what they do, and still they do it every day. They think, "If I can just improve my weaknesses, then I'll be successful." No, that's why they're your *weaknesses*. You're no good at it. Go where you're good. No one ever became a professional ice-skater by practicing the shot put. People become professional ice-skaters because they are really, really good at ice-skating.

Of course, knowing what you do well requires self-awareness. Do you know where you excel? Do you know what qualities or abilities other people would say set you apart? We cover this in depth in Chapter 7, but here's a quick example of what I mean: Say you have an amazing knowledge of trivia. This means that you've got a really good head for remembering things. What might happen if you focus that skill on a subject that intrigues you professionally? Maybe you have what it takes to become an expert in that field. That's not the same as playing Trivial Pursuit in your dad's bathrobe, while living at home at the age of 37, waiting for your parents to die so you'll get the house.

Many people spend their time in jobs or professions that don't interest them and then wonder why they struggle — why they're not advancing in their field. Most likely, they simply have not concentrated on an area or skill for which they have a strong affinity. It's tough to excel if you are overwhelmed with apathy. Let your natural passion or talent and the unique aspects of your personality help you find the right fit. Even if you are just a big guy with law enforcement fantasies who likes to get into bar fights, you'd at least make a talented bouncer. If you spend your time working hard at things you don't like, how do you feel about your accomplishments? Are you looking at life through loser-colored glasses?

What "Right" Looks Like

Do you know what the right fit for the job actually is? Years ago, I did. And my boss did not. We worked in a very successful regional office of a large corporation. The office had turned in such great numbers that the higher-ups came looking to promote someone from the regional office into a fantastic job at corporate headquarters. When opportunity knocks, some people are not dressed properly to answer the door. And in some cases, they will just stand there and talk naked.

The higher-ups came looking for my boss — on paper, anyway. They went away utterly sold on me.

My boss, who was very smart and very good at what he did, didn't believe that being viewed as the "right fit" carried as much weight as performance. He wanted to be judged on his skills, merits, and fantastic track record. The corporate folks came down to meet him, and while taking in his unshined shoes (from the Kennedy administration), his shiny and ill-fitting suits, and his long-winded explanations that he could barely stay awake for, let alone anyone else, they met me.

I was assistant regional guy to my regional guy boss, and I didn't know anywhere near what my boss knew. But I dressed well and had a good 1980s haircut. (This was the actual 1980s, so regardless of how I feel about old photographs now, my hair must have been fantastic back then.) And I explained things clearly. I could talk big picture to these corporate big-picture guys. They came for my boss but chose me.

I was not the most qualified guy for that job, that's for sure. In fact, when I got sent up to corporate, I wasn't allowed to say I'd been the assistant manager—a jump from assistant regional manager was highly irregular. I was also much younger than the person they would typically put in that position. People would come to my office, look at me, and ask to speak to Mr. Wynn. I was consistently mistaken for my own assistant. I ended up being the youngest department head in the history of the company (which led to some problems, as you'll see in a bit).

To become the right person, I'd won an unfair fight. I didn't do anything dishonest or unscrupulous to get the promotion: I looked like I fit in the corporate culture and landed the job. That's how much of the business world works. You've got to look like the right fit and make sure the people who can deliver success see you as the right fit. The truth is that I was promoted beyond my abilities; I was not mature enough for the responsibility. On the other hand, I had a totally way-cool killer job that would attract chicks.

Working the Disadvantage to Your Favor

Of course, just looking and acting like the right fit doesn't necessarily *make* you the right fit. Your appearance and performance can be boosted with an acute self-awareness, especially of some of your disadvantages. They can prepare you to cope better with the difficult people you'll meet along the way to success.

People have a hard time dealing with difficult people with whom they can't relate. They say, "What is going *on* with this person? He's unbelievable! Surely some sort of medication is in order." But if you have the self-awareness to realize how you yourself might be perceived as difficult, you can mine that awareness to handle others like you. Your jerklike disposition is now an advantage. Of course, that begs the question: Is there anything more annoying than a fully self-aware jerk? Maybe not, but you're still using your curse as a gift.

That's what I mean by turning your disadvantage into an advantage. Following are some scenarios to help illustrate my point.

The Big Ego

When I got promoted to corporate headquarters to a job possibly beyond my abilities, I was 27 years old, and all of my employees were older than I was. *"Oh yeah, young boss. I am the boss, and you are* not *the boss,"* I'd think, kind of strutting in my head.

So I go to work that first day in my new position, and I meet my people—and I actually *call* them "my people": "People, in my infinite wisdom, I will lead you to the promised land of success, where all your hopes and dreams and ideas and innovation . . . Forget all that. Because we're going to do things a special way, and that way is called *my way*. And if it's not my way, it's the highway."

Was that effective? No. They made up a special name for me — punk-ass manager. It's hard to be effective when you're punk-ass manager. So I learned a valuable lesson: If you make people feel important, you and what you have to offer are a lot more important to them. Remember: People don't choose what's best; they choose what they are most comfortable with, whether it's the best or not. Arrogance doesn't win you much favor among the well-adjusted.

But when you are in front of people with gigantic egos, your own big ego can help you navigate around everyone else's. You can manage or suppress your ego to strike a level of likability that plays to those egos. I had dinner one night with nine air force colonels. They were explaining their ability to destroy a small country over the weekend, "if they had to." Throw my self-importance in the mix, and we had what can only be described as an ego festival. To be effective in a group like that, I had to be aware of my own ego and suppress my tendency to consider myself of superior intelligence. My real goal was to survive this "Woodstock of Warlords" and be grateful these guys were on our side.

Even if it's pretty apparent that I *am* of superior intelligence (See? I still struggle on this point!), it's still advantageous not to parade my ego around. This lesson I learned during a visit to a chemical plant years ago. When I showed up, I had to watch a safety video and put on a Nomex jacket, a hard hat, goggles, and a respirator. (Note to self: Any time you visit a place that requires you to wear a respirator and a fireproof jacket, be afraid, be *very* afraid.) So I've got my respirator and armor on, and I meet Billy, who is to lead me to the administrative building. But there's a lot of construction, which appears to throw Billy.

Tentatively he says, "Okay, Mr. Wynn, just follow me." Yet he doesn't seem to know where he's going.

So I ask, "How long have you been here?"

"About 20 years."

Hmmm. Long time. Even so, I have no faith in this guy. Maybe the chemicals have seeped into his brain.

Anyway, I follow Billy into this plant, and along the way my mind replays some of the information from the safety video: One big horn blast means you're going to die; two is the all clear.

Then, as I'm walking behind Billy, I hear a long, drawn-out horn—and no second blast.

People are running past me. I'm just standing still. Billy shouts, "You! Mr. Wynn! You run that way! *That* way!" He points to where I'm supposed to run.

And I ran. I've got to hand it to Billy. He's the smartest guy I've ever known in my life, because I'm still here. Maybe Billy didn't know what I thought he should know and maybe his IQ is only in double digits, but when that horn blast went off, he knew the most important information there was.

The chemical spill that day claimed more than one life. But I got out of there alive, and Billy gets all the credit. When I arrived at the plant, I thought getting to the administration office was important. I left convinced that getting out *alive* was much more important. If I had a choice, I'd rather be alive and late than punctual *and dead*. ("We're 99 percent certain that these remains are Wynn," I can hear the medical examiner saying. "We place him just outside admin at 6:55. Just waiting on the dental records for confirmation.")

From all this I have learned that I need to be less self-important and egocentric. I need to be more tolerant of people in possession of specialized knowledge, even if they don't appear to be in possession of a *whole lot* of knowledge. Which brings me to . . .

The Know-It-All Expert

You should do three things when you face know-it-all experts. First, make sure they know that *you* know they know something. Second, paraphrase what they say. You may have noticed that pointing out their mistakes is not working for you—repeat what they say and lead them to find their own errors. Third, focus on the solution.

Know-it-all experts need to be right. Have you ever felt the need to be right? Have you ever been *so* right that nobody would talk to you?

I had a guy working for me who was responsible for 20 percent of the company's revenue; he was my miracle man, my No. 1. Everything he touched turned to success.

And one day, No. 1 was wrong. Yes, he was.

And I was right. Oh yes, I was.

So I walked up to No. 1 and looked at him in all his wrongness and he looked at me in all my rightness, and I explained with great charismatic flair how incredibly wrong he was and how incredibly right I was. I was so impactful and articulate that he agreed.

And then he quit.

He went to work for the competition. Later that week, as I was forced to clean out my desk, it dawned on me: I might want to be effective rather than being just right.

If the need to be right all the time strikes a chord with you, you possess a key element to creating an advantage. You implicitly understand something very powerful: No one wants to be wrong all the time. But building your secret advantage around this knowledge entails occasionally suppressing your own need to be right. It can be difficult to do, and Chapter 7 provides more insight and strategies for turning this disadvantage into an edge.

The Negative Thinker

Maybe you're someone who dwells on the downside of everything and points out all the problems. You can work your negativity to your advantage. (I know you're dying to say, "No, I can't!")

Think back to the description of my ideal team in the last chapter. One key player was the negative thinker who points out flaws or obstacles before the team encounters them.

Please don't confuse negative thinking with fatalistic thinking. Negativity falls somewhere between fatalism and optimism, and it has a natural and practical usefulness to it. Fatalistic thinking employs the mindset of "We could never do it. Never. Nothing can solve this problem." A sense of doom overwhelms the fatalistic thinker, not unlike what the average person feels when watching a cable news channel. Negativity, however, is a tool that's part of your thought process. It's not your total thought process. It balances the positive thinker who says, "This is great! Don't change a thing!" The negative thinker says, "This is okay, but it would be much better if we did *this*."

Negative thinking is a practical and useful survival tool. Cavemen who were totally positive and fearless are not our ancestors. They're dead. The ones who said, "Screw this. *You* fight the sabertoothed tiger! I'm outta here!"—those are our ancestors. They lived to see another day. This dissension among the ranks was part of the process of evolving and improving. It still is. It turns out worry originally developed as a survival tool, not a handicap.

Research shows that negativity serves a healthy purpose in stimulating analytical and problem-solving skills, leading to creative thinking that can improve your situation. Joseph Forgas, Scientia Professor of Psychology and award-winning researcher at Australia's University of New South Wales, compared written arguments made by subjects who were in negative and positive moods. He found that people in negative moods displayed more effective critical thinking and communication skills and were more analytical and persuasive than those who were in a positive state of mind. The study concluded that a mood of negativity "triggers more systematic, more attentive, more vigilant information processing." Wow! And I thought I was just always right and cranky.

This compares favorably to the findings of a Rice University study I cited in Chapter 1, which showed how bouts of dissatisfaction and negativity alert us to shortcomings and motivate us to work hard to identify and correct problems.

All this runs contrary to the idea that successful organizations should have no grumbling employees, no gripers, nothing but utterly satisfied people who are always in agreement, whose pores just ooze positivity and constantly spread sunshine and smiles. Let's get real. If you were fearless and had no negative thoughts, you would be naked wandering through traffic.

So, my pessimistic friend, are you beginning to see how your negativity can actually fuel your success and your team's? A lot of people have a hard time viewing negative people as productive. But some people are, in fact, negative *and* productive. What do you get when you cross Lassie with a pit bull? You get a dog that will rip your leg off and help you go find it.

The trick to offsetting this occasional ripping off of a leg is identifying and retrieving many limbs that could be even more viable. Through self-awareness, negative people can fine-tune their "disadvantage" by making it less destructive and more productive. If you're inclined to tear stuff apart, make sure you offer suggestions for putting it all back together in an even better way.

Negativity, when properly managed, can be an important component of innovation and success. This goes for the person who *is* negative and for the manager who *deals with* negative people. I don't know about you, but I can't tolerate my own bad behavior in another person for more than 10 seconds. Managing negativity is a valuable skill to have, so don't underestimate the advantage it can give you.

The Obsessive Compulsive

Our interviews with people at the top of their industries brought to light an interesting observation: Top performers often have compulsive behavior. They achieve great success but at the same time struggle with things like substance abuse or compulsive eating or have had several failed marriages.

I mentioned this to one business owner who said, "You know, I think you're onto something. My top five salespeople have got DWIs or multiple marriages and all other kinds of problems. I've got one guy who is always driving someone else's car, which is weird. But my bottom salespeople? I can't get them addicted to anything— calling people back, following up—nothing."

A guy I met in Houston told me that back in 1960 he had a meeting with Howard Hughes. He said Hughes came in with an enormous bag of pistachio nuts and ate a pistachio every second for an hour, and he didn't say a thing! Hughes is responsible for a lot of innovative things. But according to movies, biographies, and the guy I met, he was one weirdly compulsive dude. He was also one weirdly rich dude ("weirdly rich" meaning you have so much money that no one points out how weird it is that you wear gloves to shake hands).

I believe that compulsive behavior is part of being successful, but how do you turn obsessive or compulsive tendencies to your advantage? Try getting compulsive about something that will do you some good: Become compulsive about *going* to the gym rather than hanging out with your chronically unemployed friend Jim. Being compulsive about growing your business will certainly carry you further than being compulsive about watching reality TV and power-eating Fig Newtons. The key is to get into a habit that's good for you so you can let your addictive behavior lead you to success instead of rehab.

The Attention Deficient

If you have an attention deficit, heaven knows you've struggled to stick with this book. I'm impressed that you made it to Chapter 4!

Frankly, I struggle with ADD and actually lost Chapter 4 for a while, so I'm glad we ultimately found it and put it back in the book.

It's natural for us to wonder how an attention deficit could ever help us out. You think that, without focus, you cannot succeed. (And then you might lose that train of thought.) Yet our surveys put us in contact with lots of people who assist successful business owners and high-ranking corporate officers. These assistants often remarked that the driven people they work with have some attention deficit. They might not be good at digging deep and drilling down to intricate details, but they function very well as big-picture people. Frankly, those with ADD should probably avoid *all* types of drilling. That includes oil rigs and molars.

A lack of laser focus often allows a person to see how many *different* events or ventures might pan out. These people are most successful with their fingers in four or five or six ventures at a time and a lot of irons in the fire. Maybe it's that inkling of ADD that allows them to operate on a high level while delegating the details of operation and execution to others. By the way, I personally find ADD distracting.

The Insecure

I have a line of thought I call the insecurity theory, which goes something like this:

If you read the heading above and think, "Is that me? Is he talking about me?" you have just furnished solid proof that I *am* talking about you. The funny thing is that you will likely work very hard to convince me and everyone else that you're not insecure. It's convoluted, I know, but it's actually a great advantage.

Huh? How's that? Consider the short but true story of Super Realtor Bev.

Bev had won recognition as the top residential realty salesperson in the country for 22 years running. A colleague described Bev as completely driven, sleeping only four hours a night, and going far out of her way to assist clients. Then she said, "And she's *really* insecure." She explained that Bev lacks confidence but that she *projects* great confidence to clients. I heard the grinding squeak as gears began spinning in my head. (Did I just say squeaky gears in my head? I have ADD for sure.)

Throughout our interviews, we noticed that a significant number of top performers did not exude confidence when talking about their field or their achievements. Some were downright insecure. To their peers and supervisors who referred us, these star performers appeared confident, but "appear" was the operative word. We suspected that it was a bit of a show, a little outward overcompensation for something they think they lacked. The root of their success was not their outward confidence but their insecurity. If they can't bear the shame of being average, they have no choice but to be successful.

That's my insecurity theory. It's a simple proposition: If you're completely confident, wholly secure in yourself, and walking the path of Buddha, you don't need a ton of money, nor do you feel the need to be No. 1. Your ego doesn't need all that stuff. If you're 100 percent secure in yourself, how driven are you? You have no need or desire to prove yourself to the world. You can be a no-career, video-game-playing, lack-of-talent loser and still be proud of your accomplishments.

When you really feel good about yourself, I think your ego kind of fades or recedes. But if you're concerned that you're not good enough, your ego swells. It protects you and drives you forward. Many highly driven people are fueled by a belief that they might not be good enough or have all it takes to be successful. To some degree, their success comes from this insecurity, because they constantly feel that they have to prove something to themselves and others. I interviewed people who actually said they couldn't emotionally handle being poor. Some grew up poor and swore their families would have every possible advantage money could buy. I guess we know why super-rich parents buy their 16-year-olds Ferraris.

I don't know if insecurity alone can drive you to unprecedented heights. (If it can, I suppose that same insecurity has you often wondering whether you really belong there.) But combine that insecurity with some other effective traits—maybe certain skills you have in place, or a strong desire for something—and you'll likely discover a top performer. I'm not saying it's good for your psyche to be insecure; it just seems to help your bank account, based on our research. The truth is that people with the highest self-esteem are often found in prison. If you're in the big house, you need to believe in yourself just to survive lunch.

Get Yourself a Process

An attractive woman or a tall man doesn't exactly need to plot out how to use that advantage. But people looking to turn disadvantages into advantages have some work to do.

Egocentrics, for example, need to think extensively about how their egocentrism gets fed and then figure out how to apply that knowledge to feed someone else's ego. They must devote lots of willpower to minimizing their own self-importance. Maybe they inject a little self-deprecating humor into a conversation so the other party towers a little taller or shines a bit more brightly. (When people asked me how I became a person who gets consistently booked to speak at conferences, I tell them quite frankly that I have no other skills.) Or maybe they adopt a conspiratorial tone: "Don't we successful, intelligent people have a lot of inside laughs over the foibles of the common intellects?"

The point is that egocentrics must develop some kind of process to turn their disadvantage (their ego) to their advantage. In this case, the process requires some introspection, but not all do. Sometimes advantages require a focus on actions you can repeatedly take or tactics you can use over and over. Several top performers developed that kind of approach, and their revelations just might inspire you to develop your own process to help you create a competitive advantage.

Talk No Trash

My associate's mother always told her, "If you can't say something nice, don't say anything at all." I'm not sure what that says about my associate, although I'm left to imagine that she habitually fights the urge to talk trash about me. When she's silent, I start to believe that she's trash-talking me in her head. (Maybe I can add paranoia to the list of disadvantages that have brought me success.)

Mom's advice is good policy. Taken a few steps further, it just could become an advantage. It did for one of the top executives I interviewed.

The roots of Rob's advantage—the power of popularity—date back to his high school years, and he carried the advantage into his professional career, hoping it would be just as effective in the business world. He adopted a practice that nearly guaranteed he'd always be looked at positively: He made a habit of talking behind people's backs. But instead of tearing people down, he built them up, routinely making positive comments about others, knowing that the comments would spread quickly. He's the only person I've ever interviewed who could be described as sneaky *and* friendly.

Rob's strategy made him well liked, and soon everyone offered him a smile or handshake. His wall of goodwill enabled him to get the most from his coworkers. Although he was never a top performer, members of management believed that anyone this well liked must be someone they should promote to a higher level, so that's what they did over the next 17 years—from an entry-level job all the way to CEO. Rob explained in our interview: "I was told by my boss that because people were already doing what I told them and kind of reporting to me anyway, they should go ahead and put me in management. So the biggest step of my career was going from putting mail into slots to managing everyone in the mailroom. The only person who had a problem with this was the guy who was actually qualified for the job. He quit."

Rob's case drives home the point that, on some level, many aspects of life boil down to a popularity contest. If you're likable, you've got influence. Maybe it's not supposed to work that way, but it does.

This same likability factor has brought me some measure of success too. Based on my appearance and conduct around the higher-ups, I was pulled from that regional position into a job that was probably over my head. I was not movie-star handsome (although back in the day I did look pretty good with my helmet hair and skinny tie), and my conduct was not perfect, but my competition was in a $50 suit and made marketing sound like trigonometry. I came across as what the executives were looking for. There was no way they could have judged my performance except for some numbers—and, yes, the numbers were there—but my advantage came down to the fact that they liked what they saw in me. I told stories and was entertaining, and they started seeing me as an asset. My likability definitely aided in the promotion. How many managers do you think promote employees they don't like? Well, actually I did once promote a woman just to get her out of my department. So I guess her lack of ability (along with shockingly bad breath that had a range of 15 feet) was her advantage. Talk about an unfair fight: Her breath versus, let's say, the human race? Civilization had no chance.

Although likability can certainly boost your promotability, I've also learned that being personable doesn't automatically make you a great manager. But if people like your leadership style, you'll be influential. Incorporating an entertaining, likable manner into the way you interact with people can be a kind of process that, used repeatedly, can set you apart from others.

Be a Manager Who Markets

One restaurant manager I interviewed attributed his standout success to all the idiots who came before him. Compared to them, he said, he was a miracle worker.

The company had hired several people in the past with zero marketing background; they couldn't bring in the customers. When this guy took over, he sent a group of young, attractive employees to nearby restaurants and bars with the sole purpose of befriending the patrons and getting them to come to his restaurant. During our interview, he remarked, "Why develop your own clientele when you can just borrow someone else's?"

The Espionage Advantage

A guy named Jeff admitted to me that the key to his success was that he did nothing. Then he clarified. He did no work within his own business; he hired it all out. In fact, we found many leaders who delegated their work because they weren't very good at executing any one part of it. (This reinforces my earlier ADD statements.)

But Jeff also delegated to free up time to pursue his own strategy for success: He spent 45 hours a week spying on the competition. He even went in for interviews at competing venues and asked questions of management there. He was the James Bond of his industry. He actually carried a gun as well. Come to think of it, he has a very beautiful wife who just might kill him in his sleep.

A Vietnam veteran, Jeff had been shot down three times in a helicopter. He has seen hostility and does not fear being aggressive. He uses his military background and fearlessness in away that most people won't. He gets a kick out of reconnaissance, tactical planning, and aggressive takeovers. He told me that he doesn't waste time interviewing and hiring skilled or talented people; he just acquires whole companies. It's almost like he's annexing territories to fortify his position and strengthen his command over the industry. So he's not just James Bond; he's Gen. George Patton too.

Some people talk about business as war. This guy believed it! He crossed enemy lines to make sure he could win. I guess if you've been shot down a few times, gathering some industry information isn't really risky. What is there to fear if the most common injury in business is a paper cut?

Work a Dream Territory

For three consecutive years, a top salesman brought home the trophy for sales of a well-known corporation's technical software products. He repeatedly outperforms most if not all other reps across the nation. His associates marvel at his numbers, none of them suspecting that they could also turn numbers like that if they had his advantage.

Our guy started out sharing a territory that had been badly handled by several salespeople. Management brought the three existing salespeople into a meeting and fired them, leaving our guy. New to the job, he apparently hadn't had a chance to suck badly enough to get the boot, so by default he inherited the entire territory—of New York City. *Is* there a bigger market to mine single-handedly? A lack of experience was this guy's advantage! Isn't that just bizarre? His boss essentially said, "If you had more experience, we would fire you. But since you're new, we'll just give you New York."

This top performer admitted that the initial prospect of handling the biggest territory in the country was daunting; he thought he was doomed to bumble it. But then he realized three things:

1. This territory, designed for four people, was all his.
2. Because the territory was designed for four, he alone could not deliver the support and assistance his customers would expect, so he needed to rely on the sales support and tech support teams available to him.
3. He was really lucky and should buy a few lottery tickets.

He understood that he had some relationship-building to do to get the support he would need. He worked hard on that, took a deep breath, and began working his territory hard too. When he got the big trophy three years in a row, it had a lot to do with the fact that he was the only person in a territory set up to be handled by three or four people. That's a huge advantage. But the foundation of his success was his process—building good relationships to deliver the help he needed. Being lucky turned out great for him, but alone it wasn't enough; it took some strategy and work to turn that luck into success.

Surviving the Blame

Another key to being successful and influential is this: Can you survive the blame?

You might remember that I quarterbacked my high school football team. We were the worst team in the state of Florida, and I led us there. We were so bad that when we got a first down, the other team clapped. We were that bad.

As quarterback, I had a couple of distinctions you might recall: I once threw eight interceptions in a single game. The only reason I stayed in the game was because the guy who sat on the bench behind me was so bad that his passes looked more like punts (end-over-end and up for grabs).

That was a tough game in a tough season made even tougher by the fact that we had a great football program until I came. It's true. I was the beginning of the end of a great football program. It's one thing to witness the end of an era; it's another to create it.

When I'd go to school, people would say horrible things about the football team, and fights would break out over it. I came to school one time to find a mural on the wall. One panel showed my No. 11 being hanged, another showed me in a guillotine, and another showed arrows shot through me. That's how bad it was.

Through all this, I learned something: If you're the quarterback of a losing team, it's always your fault. If you're the person in charge, you're always at fault. If you throw a season's worth of interceptions in one game, don't kid yourself—it's your fault.

If you hope to some day *be* the person in charge, you had better have the kind of personality that can accept fault and bear blame. Failing that, you'd better develop an approach that allows you to at least appear to have that kind of personality. I interviewed a government manager who said that the key to his success was to have brief, clear conversations with other department heads. He described them as "hopeless idiots who could only be fired if they discharged a weapon in the building." (Let's just say that getting fired from a government job isn't that easy.) This manager's sweet-voiced assistant had great relationships throughout the bureaucracy. The manager said that as a result, and often to his surprise, people seemed to like him.

In the end, my father helped me think through an approach that would help me through all the ridicule and blame. Eventually, I learned to counter when people would jeer at me.

"Hey, Wynn! How many touchdowns are you guys gonna lose by tonight?"

"My money's on two."

I learned that if your relationships are strong enough and you don't overreact too much to what happens, you can survive the blame. It's a practical approach for handling difficult situations, and it can lift even mediocre performers to positions of success.

Put simply, a lot of leaders end up losing their jobs not because what happened was so bad but because what happened was bad *and* their relationships were bad too. The relationships were not strong enough to support them. When bad things happen to people who have the goodwill of those around them, they have a greater chance of hanging in there long enough to recover from the misstep. Surviving the blame is about the relationships you have in place. They can push you forward to achieve success even under circumstances bad enough to bring others down. A lot of people are not very good at what they do; they just have the right people supporting them and the right attitude. It's like the Rolling Stones—the band is so supportive of Mick Jagger and he has such a strong presence that we barely notice that he can't sing. And this doesn't apply to just the Stones: I heard a local rock band one night, and the guitarist, bass player, and drummer were so good and the singer so charismatic that no one cared that his voice sounded like someone killing a cat.

No One Really Craves a Fair Fight

Who wants to compete in an arena where all competitors are equally matched, where whatever success you achieve is entirely random and unpredictable? Some people do, I suppose, but that mindset doesn't produce an environment that values excellence. I understand that, in a perfect world, things in life should be as fair as possible. It also makes sense that hard work, skill, and talent should ultimately prevail. It's just that when we examined our interviews with top performers, we saw that they were more likely to have or create an advantage than to match up evenly in a "May the Best Man Win" contest.

Second-Level Lesson

Creating an advantage is possible only if you're willing to take a look at your belief system.

Are there things that you believe with all your heart that may not be true? To create an advantage, you will have to think about your limitations in a new light. Your gift may be your curse (I think I'm quoting *Spider-Man*), and it may be a valuable curse to hang on to. You may need to target an area that you view as a disadvantage and then adjust it, and your attitude toward it, in a way that allows you to use it to its full potential. If you are a person who worries that things will not work out for the best, you can use that mindset to compulsively prepare to do the best job you can. After a while, the worry is no longer stressful; instead, it becomes the drive that allows you to enjoy the benefit of your success.

I have a friend who told me that her college dance squad was "killer" until a new director decided that the squad had room for however many women showed up at tryouts. Rather than intensive screening for a dozen talented dancers, the event turned into a cattle call, blurring all distinction between a dance squad and a stampede. The result was a 50-member squad with talent that ranged from great to average to utter lack thereof.

That year, my friend flinched with embarrassment every time someone mentioned that they'd seen the squad televised during game breaks. As her major college basketball team ran all over opponents that year on its quest for an NCAA championship, during halftime performances her dance squad really just ran all over, on a quest for any sign of rhythm or coordination. "Highly televised flailing" she called it—especially excruciating on the JumboTron.

What my friend wanted was an unfair fight—a fight where advantages like being cute, moving well, and looking great in a short skirt (I never said she was humble) might actually guarantee her a spot on a team where such advantages ought to count. Instead she got a fair fight, where everyone was considered equally qualified— and everyone looked equally ridiculous.

The business world doesn't operate according to egalitarian ideas. The person with the edge gets the opportunity, the job, the promotion, and the spoils. To compete in today's world, we all need to be a bit edgy.

Remember: In the corporate world, no one wants a *fair* fight. Set up and win your *unfair* fight. Get over the word *unfair* with all its negative connotations. Get past the misconception that *unfair* means dirty, deceitful, or unethical and move on to a simple understanding: An unfair fight places competitors in an arena in which one contestant has a positive advantage that makes the battle lopsided.

If you have a positive advantage that can help you stand out, shouldn't you use it? If you don't have one, doesn't it make sense to search for one or develop one? It's like retirement; you save and prepare so you have the advantage of living comfortably without going to work every day. What if, in the name of fairness, we were not allowed to prepare for our golden years and had to keep working?

Imagine your grandmother working at Starbucks; you'd get a latte and a lecture on caffeine at the same time. We would definitely learn that time does not heal all wounds. If it did, there wouldn't be so many cranky old people walking around.

In other words, be prepared. This chapter helped you start to create an advantage in ways that are not unethical or unscrupulous. You're about to head into a series of chapters that takes you deep into exploration of where the lines are that you hesitate to cross and the reasons you've drawn those lines. Just remember this as you move forward: Your advantage is a positive thing, not to be wasted.

5

"So Your Dad Owns the Company? Nice to Meet You!"

Leveraging resources and relationships

MOST TOP PERFORMERS HAVE CREATED OR USED THEIR INNATE personal advantages (and disadvantages) to get to the top. Sure, maybe a few rode to the top on an innovative idea or two, and I suppose there are people who bought or slept their way to the top. (I've never experienced this personally, but I'm willing to learn!) But we found after talking to leaders across various industries that almost all of them have this in common: They leveraged relationships and resources to get to the top. I once heard an elderly woman say, "People who can help me have always been my favorites."

Top performers might know how to use their personal advantages to win the unfair fight, but many of them also knew someone in a position that really helped them. They worked hard to develop value in those relationships and created a platform that allowed them to forge new relationships. They just might not admit it. You never hear anyone say on the night he or she gets an award, "It's my ability to leverage lame relationships into good ones that has positioned me to succeed. I would like to thank all the borderline useless people who helped me find better people." No one would ever say that, and most people don't really think it.

For whatever reason they choose, successful people who leveraged relationships to create their opportunities often hesitate to acknowledge they've done so. Take the former *Seinfeld* scriptwriter, "Pat." As a writer, Pat clearly understood *Seinfeld's* concept of a show about nothing. In fact, the interview with Pat seemed to be about nothing as well. In the course of an hour, Pat went into great detail about comedy and capturing situational nuances on paper. When asked if there were any other details that might be interesting, Pat added, "Also, I did know Larry David back in the day."

Wait a minute. Larry David, the *producer* of *Seinfeld*? Pat may have been a great writer who deserved to be on the show's writing team, but knowing Larry David was certainly key to landing the job. Yet it took almost an hour for Pat to admit, as almost an afterthought, "I know Larry David." It was all I could do to curb my enthusiasm.

Successful people usually want to believe that what they did—their talent, skills, dedication—led to their success. After all, what kind of story is this: "Hey, you know what? I'm successful. I've done very well for myself. I built a business, and it's *alllllll* because of my brother John. John did something for me. He gave me a business, provided some start-up capital, and taught me how to run the operation. Other than that, it was all me." No one wants to say that. But many, when pressed, will admit that who they know was just as important as who they are.

Relationships and resources can expedite your ascent to the top; you just need to be willing to leverage them—to use them to your advantage. You need to identify and cultivate them to establish yourself as more valuable. Get rid of any misgivings about the fairness of doing this. To be successful, you have to leverage the relationships or resources available to you. This does not mean that you don't care about people and you're just a leechy user. It means that as you encounter people in your life and build helpful relationships, you have to let your ability to be a good friend and solution provider allow you to connect with their friends and colleagues. Some people just use their great gift of influence and clarity to create the kinds of excuses that nobody can dispute. What does that make you? A charismatic, high-impact loser.

Resources within Reach

When we asked the top residential Realtor in the United States what she did that made her so amazingly effective, she gave one of those lame answers like those we discussed in Chapter 2: People liked the way she explained things—her clients felt she understood their needs. Remember the Lynyrd Skynyrd song "Oooh That Smell. . . ."? The answer stunk. I was holding my nose while hers was growing. Millions of Realtors do the things she explained, but they're not close to her level of success.

By this point, I knew when I was being lied to. Whether she believed the line was true or not was irrelevant. (Maybe Pat wrote that line from *Seinfeld* that applies here: "It's not a lie if you believe it's true.") We pressed for more information. "No offense, but . . ." We asked her how, if her answer was the same as everyone else's, it could possibly be the reason she was the best in her field. I waited with the semidisengaged smile of a guy selling a product that didn't work. I felt like a husband finally getting the truth from his lying wife.

She lowered her voice, leaned in, and in an almost-whisper said, "For years, I had thought about my husband's list of contacts. He's the CEO of a large company, and they move people around all over the place. At some point I thought, 'You know, if I could just get that list, that would be great.' And finally, after a few years, I asked him for the list. It turns out it's okay to have it! I initially thought it was unethical, and a friend of mine thought so too." It turns out her friend was someone who put off starting her own business until she finally gave up. The strongest support you will ever get on *not* taking action always comes from those who never took action.

The Realtor had spent years with access to a personal advantage literally in bed with her, and all she did was worry about using it. You shouldn't worry about taking advantage of the people you sleep with. The closest relationships are always the easiest to leverage. But as the lessons of Lance Armstrong and Michael Phelps taught us, it is one thing to have an advantage; it is another thing to capitalize on it. Our top performer did.

She continued: "So we had this list of people who were slated to move. We knew where they lived, we knew where they were going to go, and we knew the time frame in which it was probably going to happen. So I hired a few people to help me work this list, and it was amazing what this did. And then I also started to get real estate licenses in several states." Now we know it takes more than hard work, blonde hair, and big earrings to sell houses. (I had a Realtor one time whose hair seemed much more sturdily constructed than the house she was selling.)

Well, anyway, that did it. After years of struggle, her ascent to the top of her industry was quick. And it was not just what she knew (her job) that got her there but whom she knew (her husband and the people he knew). The Realtor recognized her husband's list as a huge asset. The names and information on his list were private but available by request, and they became her personal advantage in her ascent to the top. Here's what I learned: You should always take advantage of the people you're in bed with, and don't be afraid to go for their privates.

What people and resources do you have access to through the people you know? For some, the resources might even be easy to come by. The real challenge is leveraging them to achieve your desired outcome while providing real value.

Who's Your Daddy?

Sometimes success comes from not wasting your resources. According to one of Paris Hilton's former publicists, Hilton wanted to increase her celebrity exposure. I cannot imagine that there was ever a time there was anything left of Paris Hilton to expose, but back then I guess the crowd at the bars and parties she attended weren't in a position to advance her aspirations as a model and actress. So she used her family's wealth to hire members of the paparazzi to follow her and snap photographs. The shots generated exposure in local newspapers and the tabloids and soon created the celebrity buzz she sought.

She may be blonde, yes. But dumb? Not so much. She leveraged the resources she had and truly embodies the phrase "fake it till you make it." No kidding—I'm impressed and I think everyone else should be too. To just one day get bored with the mundane opportunities of trust-fund folly and say, "You know, I think I want to be famous," and then actually do it is not that common. Becoming a celebrity based on talent is tough enough; to do it without any is damned near impossible. It can lead people to wonder "Who's your daddy?" Of course, in Hilton's case, the phrase "Who's your granddaddy?" is more accurate, albeit a tad creepy.

Consider Hollywood as a whole. Studios and production companies may produce entertainment that provides us with escape, but it is big business, and the rules of business apply. Actors need all the leverage they can get to break in and get a shot at success. The glossy magazines and gossip mills would have you believe that it is all good looks and talent and sex that make actors successful. Well, these don't hurt, but there are plenty of good-looking, gifted, bed-hopping actors looking for a shot in Hollywood.

The truth is that many actors' paths to success are paved with nepotism. Gwyneth Paltrow's mother is Blythe Danner, who has made more films than Gwyneth. The late Bruce Paltrow, Gwyneth's father, wrote and produced many successful TV shows and movies such as *St. Elsewhere* and Gwyneth's *Duets*. Nicolas Cage's real last name? Coppola. As in Francis Ford Coppola, who created *The Godfather* and more. He's Cage's uncle. Drew Barrymore, Robert Downey Jr.—the list is long, and that's just blood bonds. The list could fill this book if you added marriage and other relationships.

If you watch the Biography Channel, you might notice another common trait among actors and comedians: The vast majority of them come from upper middle class or wealthy families. You hear things like, "After wrecking his father's yacht and dropping out of Dartmouth's theater program, he finally got his first break." What? When I was doing stand-up on the road and mingling with other comedians, it was rare that someone came from humble means, and that includes me. Even Larry the Cable Guy (Daniel Whitney) graduated from a private high school in Palm Beach County, Florida. I'm pretty sure he had sleeves on his shirt back then.

Actors, like most professionals in other industries, don't like to admit to these resources, but their stories are not exceptional. I interviewed a businessman who had reached a high level of success, though he landed just outside the top 1 percent. When prodded for his secret, he said, "My dad gave me a whole lot of money and said, 'Hang on to it, son.' And I did." Unlike his brother, who'd been endowed with a similar trust fund, this guy hadn't squandered his.

The lesson is simple. If you are born with an advantage in resources, don't give it up. Life deals some people better circumstances than others. There is nothing wrong with having money. We can't choose the family we're born into (although someone who clearly had a bad childhood wrote a book that says you can). Remember, life is not fair. The human race likes to give the impression that being the underdog and/or poor is somehow noble. That's because people have forgotten what the definition of noble really is: possessing hereditary rank in a political system or social class derived from a feudalistic stage of a country's development. In other words, nobles were medieval trust-fund babies with every extreme advantage you could have except big-screen TVs and indoor plumbing.

There is nothing underhanded about using these advantages to create opportunities. Yet people with these resources can be careless. Any resource or relationship must be appreciated for the advantage it gives. The key to using it successfully is being a good steward of whatever opportunities it provides. For those of you who grew up poor, you have the big advantage of knowing what a lack of success actually feels like. People always say that they learned a lot growing up poor, but they rarely admit what they actually learned—that being poor sucks and being successful is worth utilizing every advantage you have.

Your Loser Buddies

If you're not born with connections, you can manufacture them. But first you have to make some room for them.

Start by thinking about whom you know. The most successful people spend time with people who can position them to succeed. If you're hanging out with your loser buddies, what's that doing for you? I guess it makes you feel better. Hanging out with the guy who still has that car from high school naturally makes you feel successful. However, if you're hanging out with people who are much more successful than you are, you might *be* a loser buddy! Still, it's better to be a loser buddy pulled up by winners than it is to be dragged down by your loser buddies. It's important to spend time with people who can actually help get you where you want to go. If you're spending time with people who cannot position you to succeed, you don't have time for the people who can.

An old adage says that you've got to stick with the horse that brung ya. Well, maybe that horse has gone as far as it can go, or it might have been the wrong horse to begin with. In either case, it's time to switch horses. You've got to be willing to do things that will get you where you want to go.

In the late 1990s, I was not spending my time wisely. I met this incredible woman, and the good chemistry between us was more than I had ever experienced. I was just crazy about her, and she was just crazy! She was fun, cute, and clearly out of her mind. I had to break up with her, and it was not easy. Apparently, there is a fine line between being really fun to be with and screaming, "Help me get my date off the roof of this night club!" Eventually I learned how amazing your love life can be when you stop dating the mentally ill.

Laura, the owner of a fabric store chain, had a similar experience, not with a person but with her cherished secondhand 1950s-era cash register. Well, not exactly. You almost never have to bail a cash register out of jail, but you see where I'm going. She bought it when she started her business. It weighed a ton, had that old-fashioned glass bar across the top that displayed the amount owed, and dinged when the cash drawer opened. To Laura, each ding symbolized her success—the empowerment she felt in starting a business when women didn't run many businesses. It embodied her good business sense and the love of a loud and proud cha-ching.

But by the early 1990s, the nostalgic power of Laura's machine was hindering her success. Cash registers were now computers. Her old-fashioned machine was quaint but made her well-established business outdated. Not to mention the fact it could give you a heart attack if you were too close to that thing when it went off. With a heavy heart, she ditched the behemoth and invested in equipment that could take her where she was going, not remind her of where she had been. The new equipment meant growth and new capabilities for managing her books, tracking her inventory, and more. The old register had become a tool version of the loser buddy, complete with unnatural noises and an out-of-date fashion sense. Whatever its beauty and symbolism, it offered no personal advantage and prevented her from capitalizing on customer information.

I'm not saying that you should desert your friends, especially those who helped you along the way or those whose company you enjoy. But too many people remain committed for life to people who take them nowhere. Successful people grow past old relationships. They constantly evaluate their connections and ask, "Is my life going to go where I want it to go if I'm attached to this person?" It's a completely unnecessary risk, like skydiving. Why would I jump out of a perfectly good airplane just to see if I'm not killed? Now if that plane's on fire, I'm the first guy out! Some people like taking risks, it's true. But our research showed that the most successful people will take risks that have a bigger payoff than just survival.

Also, we don't owe our lives to people who were once good for us but now make us miserable. It's like energy drinks and aging. When you're young and on the go, you need something to keep you going—some sort of caffeinated ginseng boost that gets you wired and ready to pounce on prosperity. But when you're older, that same drink makes you cranky, gives you the jitters, and causes you to mow your lawn at midnight. Maybe you achieved a lot with the help of that energy drink, but at some point it's time to give it up. Your life belongs to *you* regardless of all the help you've had along the way.

You should be grateful, return the favor, if possible—and, if need be, run like hell.

Call it self-preservation. If people you know are always depressed or complaining, it's hard to be around them—it's draining! And if you're spending time with them, you're not spending time with people who can position you well or using resources that can advance you. People are not effective in situations when they can't take that close look at what's best for them. Can you really be effective or do what you need to do if you don't take care of yourself?

It's like when flight attendants tell you that in the event of loss of cabin pressure—which is bad because if they tell me we've lost cabin pressure, odds are I hear nothing they say after that—the oxygen mask will drop down. These are clearly just plastic cereal bowls with rubber bands on them, but on a plane they're lifesavers. And the flight attendants tell you that if you're traveling with a child, you need to put your mask on before your child's. That's because dead parents generally have poor parenting skills. You cannot help your child if, in fact, you are no longer breathing.

Sometimes, especially in business, we have to take care of ourselves first, or we're dead. We must be willing to sever relationships that hold us back and forge new ones that move us in the direction we want to go. Is this selfish? Absolutely. But it's effective and essential. When we looked at our top performers, they all had this certain level of selfishness. They said, "I want to be successful more than I want to hang out with you. Nothing against you and your loser ways, but I have got to go." That makes a lot more sense than saying, "What else can I do for you that will prevent me from achieving my life's goals?"

An older man with a rural mindset (okay, he was a hick) offered me the greatest advice I ever heard about goal-setting: "You know, if you want to be a good guitar player, you ain't gonna get there carving wooden ducks." Excuse me? Obviously, this man spent a great deal of time alone in the woods, possibly with some carvings that thwarted his music career. But his point was solid, and I was ready to hear it. He meant that if you want to be a good guitar player, you have to spend a lot of time practicing the guitar. So ask yourself: Are you carving ducks, or are you practicing your guitar? Are you doing something right now that is going to get you where you want to go? Ditch the loser buddy and the horse you rode in on and find and develop new ones that further your goals.

The Three-Level Process for Creating and Leveraging Relationships

A husband-and-wife team running a small, struggling business casually befriended an older man who operated a competing business in the same market. Their ideas were innovative, but he was well established in the community and had the loyalty of longtime customers. As their relationship developed, this man became too old to manage his operations, and his children had no interest in taking over the family business. Knowing this, the older man turned to his nice friends at the competition and offered, more or less, to turn his successful business over to them.

The husband and wife seized the opportunity to combine their novel ideas with his long-term customers and good standing. They merged companies and then chose to use his name. They knew his name mattered, not theirs. A lot of small business owners make the mistake of believing the illusion that their company name has power over a more established brand. If you go to places like Branson, Missouri (the kind of place you go if your career dies and you're still alive), you see signs promoting performers you have never heard of with the phrase "world famous" in front of their names. I often think, "What world? Do you mean Earth? Maybe this guy is huge on Venus, but he's not really famous on our planet."

The husband-and-wife team understood that "Branson branding" would not work for them so they took action. They did not get hung up on their egos and the name on the door. They approached the relationship from a purely business perspective, analyzing what would give them the most leverage in the community. The older man was very grateful, and they stayed close until his death. A large picture of him hangs in the lobby of the office with the caption "Our Founder."

This is not something successful people freely admit. Who wants to admit that their success is all because of someone else's contribution? But this partnership happened only because (1) the couple needed what this guy had to be successful and (2) he needed the support his family would not give him. They both received value from the partnership and were satisfied with the results of their relationship.

I guess a big lesson here is that you should always be really nice to elderly rich people. But you don't have to wait for your toughest competitors to die to capitalize on the relationship. Speed the process! (That does *not* mean you should kill them!) Get intentional about striking up relationships with people who position you to make a stronger impression. Know what you want to achieve and direct your energy toward the relationships you need to make or strengthen. From our research, we created a fairly simple three-level process based on techniques used by people who were good at leveraging relationships. And it's much better than waiting for someone to take a dirt nap.

Level One: Get Them to Listen to You

If the person whose relationship I need to leverage is inside an organization I want to do business with or this person knows someone

I want to know, that's a good start. But that relationship still must be powerful enough to yield the opportunity or relationship I need. That is the definition of leverage.

Let's say that you have a contact within a company who has no real influence with the exception of getting you to buy lunch. We interviewed top-performing networkers and leaders who could get things done in times of change and discovered a pattern that again was beyond charisma, position, and intelligence. To get fully footed on level one, you have to get that person—the one who is not the person you know but the person correctly positioned to help—to listen and trust you. I don't just mean that this person hears you. He or she has to *listen* to what you have to say, understand what you mean, and then work with you to create the new relationship. The way to do that is to give this person what everyone wants: love, money, and prestige.

I don't mean literally; I mean love (sincerity), money (offering multiple solutions), and prestige (making people look good in front of the people they want to impress).

Love. Does your sincerity match the situation? If you're not sincere enough, people think you're cold. If you're overly sincere, people think you're a fake.

I knew a guy named Carmine who sold heavy equipment. He told me, "I'm a real closer. As a matter of fact, I'll let you know, if you don't sign on the dotted line, things may not go so well for your family." He tended to yell at people and do things that made him come off as cold. He was good at what he did, but he struggled because he did not come across as sincere enough.

On the other hand, Sharon, a clerk at an upscale women's boutique, gushed every time a client came out of the dressing room. One day, a two-week postpartum mother named Sue walked in and said that she had gained 60 pounds during her pregnancy but had a formal affair for which she needed a dress. Dress after dress, Sharon told Sue she looked great. "That was made for you!" she raved. "I've never seen you look better; that fits you perfectly!"

Sue fumed as she thought, "Did she really just tell me I've never looked better than *this* point in my life? I've never been heavier except for two weeks ago, when the kid inside me actually *counted* for some of this weight! She might as well just tell me that this dress comes in three sizes: big, huge, and 'Oh my God, it's moving toward us!'"

Sue thus believed two things: If I've truly never looked better, how horrible do I usually look? *And* if, as I suspect, I have indeed looked better, Sharon will say anything for a sale.

Even lines like "You look fantastic!" come off as completely insincere when your customer is thinking, "No, I don't. I have mirrors at the house that tell me I'm big and bloated. Stop angling for the sale and give me the facts. I need a whale costume made from attractive fabric."

Being overly enthusiastic does not mean that you lack sincerity. But Sharon's overly sincere approach came off as fake. Compare her with Gina, a jewelry saleswoman in Texas. Gina gushes too, but she does it sincerely. The storeowner told us that Gina had generated better sales numbers than all the other salespeople combined because she makes the experience personal. Gina greeted all customers warmly and openly. For repeat customers, she'd immediately say, "I have a piece of jewelry that I've been thinking about for you!" For new customers, she'd start a conversation before selling, getting a sense of who they are before determining which pieces of jewelry would be appropriate for them. With her smooth south Texas drawl and her drawn-on, high-arcing, Joan Crawford eyebrows, she always seemed glad and consistently surprised to see you.

The difference between Sharon and Gina was that Gina kept it real. Her sincerity ran deep. She truly believed what she told her clients. Her philosophy was that jewelry either works on a person or it doesn't. Certain personalities can carry a particular look, and she learned to identify a person's jewelry style, directing him or her to what worked and volunteering the news when it did not. In our interview, she said, "Sometimes people would say they really loved a piece, and I would have to tell them, 'Honey, I love that piece too—just not on you.'" Then, she would quickly show another design and praise the match between the stone and the customer. I call this the sandwich approach: bad news served between two tasty slices of good news.

Thus, words like "fantastic" that sounded empty and desperate coming from Sharon were sincere coming from Gina. Her approach catapulted her to a position of success because her sincerity matched her beliefs and suited her situation. Gina in her own words was "about as real as you can get, sugar."

We trust people because we know they're being who they are. That's why we connect with people like Gina who are real characters. We know that they are who they are wherever they go; they're genuine. We'll let a real character get away with things we won't let others get away with. Imagine the outraged owner of an auto repair shop storming into the garage to ask, "What happened to the tools in the shop!?" "Oh, Jimmy got drunk and stole them last night. He'll bring them back. You know Jimmy." Indignation fades where real characters are involved, because there's an underlying genuineness and trust there that no one questions.

The lesson is important: Being genuine and sincere earns you trust. If you are as cold as Carmine, don't think suck-up Sharon's approach will help. Make sure people trust your sincerity in the relationships you're trying to cultivate. In fact, Carmine would be as effective selling dresses to postpartum women as Sharon but would make a far better reality TV show.

Money.   If you're the kind of person who says there's only one way to do something, you compromise your ability to influence others. Most people—especially those under 35 years of age who grew up with computers—know that every problem has more than one solution. If you insist on just one way, you've got no depth of value. People will think you lack the conviction to consider other options, and they'll question your intelligence.

You are better off—it is even preferred—offering that there is more than one way to accomplish a task. What's the worst thing that happens? People don't use your idea? They say you're wrong? At least no one will question your ability to think and innovate. And they are pretty sure you are not an idiot. A safety director for an oil company said it best: "There are three ways you can do this; two of them will kill you. I like it this way, the way that won't kill you."

He went on to explain, "One day we might do it another way. Today is not that day. We may do it that way in the future, so keep bringing us information because that's where innovation comes from. Right now, we're going to do it the way that has the best track record. It doesn't mean that your way is wrong. It's just not what we're going to do right now."

A woman in Florida is the living embodiment of offering multiple solutions for a single problem: She's a veterinarian and a taxidermist. Her motto is: "Either way, you're getting your dog back."

Prestige.   Okay, you've given the love and showed them the money; now let them know that you'll make them look good in front of the people they want to look good in front of. They'll listen to everything you say *every* time you open your mouth for the rest of your life. That's the power of positioning. It's why some people are so effective despite little knowledge, talent, and intelligence, while other people who have all the information, skills, and brains go nowhere forever. It's why it took so long to get seatbelts in cars but the Pet Rock (literally a rock in a box) was green-lighted at the first meeting. It is about creating your own advantage by the way you lay a foundation of influence.

Can you make people look good in front of the people they want to look good in front of? Can you make people look smart? Can you make the husband look good in front of the wife? The boss look respectable in front of the employees? The employees shine for the boss? It's a lot easier to make some people look smart than others, but the payoff is huge.

Jennifer, the assistant director of a training organization for 13 years, was a master at making other people in her nonprofit look good, which was important because this particular organization put the "non" in nonprofit. The organization needed to make sure its employees felt rewarded to compensate for the nonpaycheck they got every two weeks. During weekly conference calls that included all 11 members of the organization's team, Jennifer would mention with sincerity how well an employee's idea had worked or how quickly someone had accomplished a difficult task. She did not overdo it but rather matter-of-factly made sure that this person felt the love. She combined love and prestige by sincerely complimenting a person's efforts while praising that person in front of not only the director but all other members of the team. I call that the machine-gun prestige approach. Regardless of your aim, everybody was hit because you fired a lot of ammunition into a crowd. (Forgive me for making praise sound so dangerous.) As a result, all the team members liked accomplishing tasks for her because they knew they would be recognized for their efforts. And her bosses noticed her because she was able to get so much accomplished in a very profitable way.

Remember, the most effective, fastest, and easiest way to achieve level one in leveraging a relationship is through love (sincerity), money (offering multiple solutions), and prestige (making people look good in front of others). Anyone who makes people look bad, gets stuck on that one solution, or comes off as fake or cold or weird will lose business time and again to a competitor who delivers the love, money, and prestige. When was the last time you heard someone say, "I've thought it over, and I'm definitely going with the fake, stubborn dude who makes me look bad in front of my boss"? And truth be told, phony, inflexible humans who make people look bad in front of others make up a large portion of the business world.

Love, money, and prestige are the foundation for establishing trust within your relationships. You have stacked the odds in your favor and won the first round of the unfair fight. Even if the other person has a better idea than you, the powers that be are going to come to you and say, "Can you please use his idea?" I was in a consulting think tank with other so-called experts whom I did not know well. I was the only person in the room without a Ph.D. or an engineering degree. At the end of the day, the CEO pulled me aside and said, "You are the only one who did not tell us how wrong and stupid we are. If I hire these other guys, my staff will freak. Can you help us do what they said needed to be done?" I said, "Yes, sir, but I'll have to hire one of those other guys to help me." He said, "No problem, as long as he does not come back in the building."

Level Two: Your Specific Value Proposition

Level two requires you to graduate from developing trust to proving you have value. You need to create your specific value proposition. You've got to identify a problem, show a solution, and then demonstrate why that solution has value. A solution without value is like being on a double date with your parents; sure, you wanted to go on a date and you achieved that. It's just that the longer the date lasts, the less you value relationships as a whole. A lot of people aren't very good at showing value because they don't understand what I call issue-action-impact. The issue is the problem; the action is the solution; the impact is why the solution has value. If you can explain it that way—here's the problem, here's the solution, here's why the solution has value for you—then you will be seen as having value. You've *proven* that you and your solution have value. You are actually part of the solution. And if you are not part of the solution, it means that people can have what they need and not need you.

For example, every car salesperson wants to sell you a car, but top car salespeople think about the value of that car (beyond just sticker price). The best salespeople want you to believe that a particular car will make your life *better*—that their solutions have higher value propositions. After all, you could buy any number of cars, and the salesperson already knows your problem: You need a car. The solution? I'm going to sell you *this* car because I've taken time to ask the relevant questions and I think *this* car suits you. Why does that solution have value? You need this car to be effective: It's fuel-efficient and comfortable during your long commute, it's roomy enough to accommodate your growing family, and it looks classy enough that you're not embarrassed to take clients to lunch in it. If you don't have this car, you waste money, you dread your commute, and you make your family and clients uncomfortable. So I haven't just sold you a car; I've explained to you why that car is so important to you, based on your needs. And you see me as an informative resource rather than the slick car salesperson who takes your offer into a secret office and convenes with an imaginary manager.

In other words, top performers aren't successful because they believe that the solution stands by itself. ("I've got a great solution; if my solution is good enough, I win.") The truth is that the impact of that solution is really more important. To gain leverage with or within a company, you must show people at the company the same thing that the car salesperson demonstrated: how what you do (or sell) would be of value to them. Good ideas are not good enough anymore; those days are gone. People are narcissistic, and everybody who can Google has a good idea these days. People like the things that personally benefit them. Value is personal; solutions are not.

To demonstrate your value, you need to identify a problem that the company has, offer something *different* as a solution, and then show people at the company the impact of *your* solution—the personal value to a specific demographic. It's like selling software. It does not have to be better, and in many cases it's worse. It just has to be upgraded with a new look and have all the cool things that geeks desire. Software is not necessarily designed for the end-user. It's designed by geeks to impress the other geeks, who sell it, maintain it, and revel in its complexity. If you are wondering why they can clone sheep these days but your new software is slower, now you have your answer. Software gets more ambitious but not always better.

Impact is whatever the people you are trying to target believe has the most impact. You can't influence people unless you know what they value. Maybe it's something different from the thing they tried years ago that didn't work then and won't work now. They need better buy-in from their employees and greater credibility, especially among those employees who saw management's current proposed solution tank way back when. Those employees have little faith in the direction they're being taken right now. Show how you can fix that, and you will be lord of the geeks and the end-users with a very happy flock of cloned sheep.

Where do you start your quest for contacts who can uncover the problems that need action and establish what will have value? Whether it's a small company or local association or a multibillion-dollar, multinational corporation, it's always an advantage to try to leverage someone who has been there a long time. History, regardless of title or personal performance, gives people insight and knowledge; they often know things that no one else knows. And the source can be quite unexpected and, in some cases, pretty darned weird.

Kenny, a consultant working with a large company, was talking to the company's employees to discover information and identify problems. He unearthed a key issue the company had been grappling with for years—employee dissatisfaction and turnover—by talking with the janitor. What? The guy with the mop and bucket? The person I don't say hello to because I'm afraid I'll sound condescending? The guy responsible for all those murders in low-budget high school horror films? That's my key killer contact?

The janitor had been with the company for 36 years and often overheard people's conversations. "These guys are invisible," Kenny said during our interview. "The janitor knows that the change the company is instituting now was attempted 30 years ago. It didn't work then, and those employees who have been there 30 years know it will not work now."

The janitor provided Kenny with insights and information that few other people in the company had. And it was an issue that the company had been facing for a long time. Kenny had the key information he needed. He had identified the problems and figured out what the company valued so he could have influence—all from the janitor. The cleanup man knew where all the company secrets were buried (and maybe a few bodies as well).

Level Three: Confiding in You

If you're getting the information you need, you've reached level three—confiding in you. At level three, your contacts will tell you the truth about what's blocking their progress or anything else you need. You know you've reached this level when people start to give you the dirt. They say things like "This company is really screwed up, and I'll tell you why. The real problem is Don over there in accounting. He's not really good at—how should I say it?—math."

When your contacts are confiding in you, that's when you can say, "I know that you know Bill, and he's kind of high up in the company. You think maybe he could be helpful in this situation? Would you invite him to lunch so that we can talk about this?" That's a lot better than saying, "Look, you are not as valuable as Bill, and I don't want to die of old age waiting for your career to take off. So can we go to lunch with Bill?" But it does not matter what you say if you're not at level three. When you reach the third level, you have the leverage to make things happen.

Guaranteed you'll get your lunch and the relationship you want. Because he or she is confiding in you, the two of you are now close enough so that you can pop the question. Can we now move forward? Yes! Can we now bring somebody else into the relationship? Yes! Until people are confiding in you, your leverage is minimal and you run the risk of asking for a meeting that you're not really valuable enough to attend.

People confide in you because they trust you. If they don't trust you, they're not going to risk their position, standing, and image within the company by introducing you to a higher-up in the company. They'll think you'll just screw up. It's like when you are a kid and your mother asks you to take your little brother with you to your very popular friend's house. Your little brother would have to prove pretty valuable to keep you from using your bicycle lock to tether him to a tree before you go inside. The fear is that he'll blurt out some embarrassing family secret before you can kill him!

So once you've achieved that third level, you can ask for that meeting with that key person you want to meet. This is more effective than bringing in sandwiches or employing some other gimmick to get you in front of other people in the company. But a lot of people won't do it. People typically won't leverage one relationship for another. They'll object because they think it's manipulative.

But it's not.

We leverage relationships every day, even without thinking about it. The most common way people meet spouses is through family and friends. Isn't that a leveraged relationship? I recently read an article that showed the best and worst places to meet a future spouse. It's no surprise that the best place was through family and friends. (The worst place was any kind of 12-step meeting.)

A friend of mine went to the movies with her family to see *Ironman*. The movie was too dark and graphic for her 9-year-old son, but her 11-year-old and her husband wanted to stay. She took her younger son to the ticket counter to exchange their tickets for another flick. The attendant lacked the authority (and apparently the willingness) to make the exchange, which is not uncommon; a counter worker once told me she was paid not to resolve problems but just to apologize—and then she said, "And I'm really sorry about that."

Because of my friend's sincerity, the clerk had no qualms about bringing in the manager when my friend appealed to take the issue to someone at a higher level who had the authority to resolve the situation. That is leveraging a relationship in its basic form: This person could not give me what I wanted but she knows someone who can. I just need to leverage this person in the right way to get to that other person. Of course, the manager exchanged their tickets, and they went to see a different movie, and everyone was happy. This is not the only way that movie theaters mirror life. Some things that are supposed to be okay for kids are clearly not. (PG–13 means there will still be profanity and sexual situations but only from really attractive people with good intentions.)

We leverage relationships in our social lives all the time. Yet we sometimes hesitate to do it in a business environment. And when we do, we hesitate to admit it as if it minimizes our success. But Pat, the talented comedy writer at the beginning of this chapter, might still be waiting for that breakthrough success if a relationship hadn't come into play. Pat scored a major sitcom only after reestablishing contact with an influential friend from the past and then leveraging that relationship. And by the way, Larry David made a few key connections in his previous job as a limo driver in New York City.

First-Level Lesson

The willingness to take a relationship you have and turn it into one that connects you to someone who has more value is one of the cornerstones of success and influence.

Some people are afraid to do this because they think it's manipulative. Don't let someone tell you that the resources you have are not okay to use. You get to make that decision.

Second-Level Lesson

The powerful people and opportunities of the world are available only to those who can combine value with trust.

You have something that can provide value to the people or relationships you're leveraging, and they trust that you will view that value the way they do. They know that if they bring you into their world, you will reflect well on who they are, and this usually means that you agree with them on what is most important.

When it comes to leveraging relationships at the highest levels, you've got to look at who has influence and connect with them. Yet many companies are like ivory towers, and that presents problems. There are departments within the same company in which people don't know each other at all; they aren't connected except for the fact that they're in the same company directory. So communication between business silos can be nonexistent. Our research showed that the big problem that no one was willing to address is that change does not move well in most organizations, because departments do not know or actually doubt the value of each other.

The key is to find someone in another department who is influential and educate this person on your value. Then you can leverage that relationship and establish a communication link. If you can do that with all the departments, then your department works wonderfully because you have the connections and relationships in other departments to get the things you need. That's why some department managers or department heads are so extraordinarily effective—because they have leveraged those relationships around them and as a result they have the resources they need to be effective and successful.

Are you connected to people who are influential? Or are you reading this waiting for your loser buddies to join you for a beer? (They'll show, if you're buying.) A lot of us are connected to a lot of people, *none* of whom have influence. Too many of those connections soak up time you could otherwise devote to achieving your goals. The goal of your loser buddies is to get you to see that your ambitions are not what's most important; it's your commitment to not leaving them behind. People who are not successful do not want you to judge them on their actions but on who they believe you really are, which is just like them—no better and no more deserving. If you don't want to be part of the growing loser movement, leverage a few relationships and see what happens.

6

The Truth about Success

Being the best versus being consistently chosen

Success doesn't typically fall in your lap just because you have a look, a plan, or a resource at your disposal. There are good-looking people who know important people, have a great vision, and totally suck at everything they get their little loser hands on. To use your personal advantage to *its* best advantage, you must understand the business world in which you operate.

Success in today's business culture rests upon some strong truths, ones that often contradict our existing assumptions about things like fairness. Succeeding in today's business culture requires that we acknowledge these truths despite those assumptions. Anyone who does this will have a solid understanding of behaviors that influence people, and that's the gateway to fertile ground for success. And it goes beyond just developing a personal advantage.

As you know, I started my research looking for the attributes, skills, and behaviors that elevated people to the very top of their field. I sought common ground among uncommon individuals—the shared traits, practices, skills, or behaviors that separated the top 1 percent from all others. Of course, I ended up discovering deeper truths about the secret advantages that provided the foundation for this book. But we also discovered some universal, illuminating truths about business in those interviews that have important implications. Understanding these truths allows top performers to optimize their personal advantage and create opportunities.

So, what do the top 1 percent do consistently or understand implicitly that makes them so effective? That is the foundation of this particular chapter, and our research came down to six important observations:

- People are most likely to bond with people who listen more than they talk.
- People are most likely to agree with people who do not make them feel wrong.
- People are most likely to value a solution they helped to create.
- People are most likely to abandon a complex process, even if it works.
- People are most likely to choose what they're comfortable with, whether or not it's the best.
- People are most likely to follow leaders who make them feel important; those leaders are most likely to elicit the best performance.

These observations all point to the power of influence being seated in trust, clarity, and comfort. This chapter explores all six observations, starting with the first three that intertwine to create what I call the *building blocks of trust*.

Influence Factors: The Truth about Trust

Conventional wisdom on trust says that building trust takes time. But when we looked closely at the research, we found that trust building wasn't a slow, progressive, cumulative process at all. Time was not a major factor. After all, you've got people who've known you for five years who still don't trust you, and you have people who've known you for five minutes who do.

Trust is built on a foundation of two things: compassion and competence. Do people know and feel you really care about them, their future, their well-being, or whatever is important to them? Do they think you can do your job however they believe that's defined (which is probably based on how well you have consistently defined it)? If they believe those two things, they'll trust you pretty quickly.

So, how do you prove to someone in a very short period of time that you really care and can do the job? We looked at thousands of interviews with employees and customers to discover specifically what competence and compassion look like to them. They said with overwhelming frequency:

- I felt heard.
- I felt listened to.
- The encounter was collaborative.
- I could see my input in their solution as proof of being heard.

Well, I was not impressed. All this research to find out that "I need to feel heard" is the root of people's trust in you? But my staff emphatically—and ironically—told me I wasn't *hearing* what people were telling us. (I'm much more compassionate and competent now.) I was sitting on this giant body of information that showed that if people feel heard in the first minutes of a conversation, they tend to trust you automatically and they don't even know why. That's why the guy sitting next to you on the plane can talk your ear off and at the end of the flight believe you are his best friend. He loves and trusts you; you could take him or leave him (or maybe just leave him and take Xanax).

The pure power of making people feel heard is the foundation of earning trust.

Listening for Positioning

Whatever you're selling—a product, a management style, a strategy, a solution, an idea—people are more likely to buy it if you listen more than you talk.

How can listening have such power? Because we stink at it. Humans just don't listen well, a disappointing fact that makes those who do listen stand out. According to the International Learning Association, we are distracted, preoccupied, or forgetful about 75 percent of the time that we are "listening." Phillip Hunsaker and Tony Alessandra, in their book *The Art of Managing People*, propose that a lack of learned listening skills might be the simplest source of our poor listening habits. The way I see it, from birth to age five, humans acquire more knowledge than they'll learn for the rest of their lives. If they do not feel heard in those formative years, they won't possess the ability to listen well. Listening is not hereditary; it's very difficult to listen if you feel no one listened to you. I'm the first to admit it; it's hard to listen to children. My daughter once asked if she could have a tattoo. I said, "No! Because you're in kindergarten." Nothing screams bad parenting like a tattooed five-year-old.

So some of us can trace our abysmal listening skills to childhood, but even the most skilled listeners among us encounter barriers they must work through.

Barrier 1: Being Preoccupied Sometimes our own thoughts or preoccupations get in the way. I once hired a real go-getter who, by the second day on the job, began explaining how he intended to revamp everything. As he went on and on, I felt my focus slipping from his ideas to his appearance. "Look at the size of this guy's head," I thought. "It's like a giant Muppet head!" Then I noticed he had black hair, blond eyebrows, and a red mustache. I apparently hired Mr. Potato Head and did not know it. I could not bounce back from that thought process to concentrate on what he was telling me.

Barrier 2: Tuning Out When somebody starts talking about all the same old wants and needs and problems and issues, we try to listen and be there for them but in reality we start thinking, "I wish you would just shut up!"

Typically, that's how we rob people of their uniqueness. Leaders do it, salespeople do it, housewives do it—everybody does it. People tell us they've got a problem, and we think, "That is *not* a problem!" So we tune it out or, worse, we actually say, "That's not a problem." What do they do in response? They make their problem look a lot worse or urgent so we'll pay more attention to it. Some people will actually go out and sabotage something to prove there's a problem, as if to say, "Oh, it's not a problem? I just set it on fire. Is it a problem now?" You've now increased the size of the problem by telling people their problems are *not* problems. Also when you tell people their problems are not important, they feel they are being called stupid. You cannot influence or move forward with anyone you have made to feel stupid. It's nearly impossible to earn the trust of someone you've effectively just called an idiot.

Barrier 3: A Predisposition Not to Listen There's a story I tell about what my teenager once said to me: "Dad, I've made a decision. I'm going to dye my hair green, I'm going to get a neck tattoo, and I'm going to get my ear pierced." Now, if I could push past how irked I already was at how this kid looks, it might have sunk in that a body piercing in the *ear* was a somewhat disturbing request coming from this teenager. But that detail was lost on me as I inspected this child, taking it all in—the demands, the shirt that ends three inches above the skirt (are these two clothing items coming back together again at some point?), the fishnet stockings. I said, "Son, there's no way you're leaving the house like that."

When a person's appearance or behavior is completely alien to us, we often struggle to look past the exterior and get to the real content. I call this the problem of intellectual diversity: when people have a way of thinking that's tough to understand because it's so different from ours. We don't hear what people are saying because we just don't *get* them. We don't understand their behavior, their philosophy, their culture, and we can't get past it.

Mainstream examples of this surface in offices every day. People from operations and marketing often have trouble communicating because of their different ways of thinking. The marketing department thinks the operations people don't have a clue about what's important, and operations people think the marketing people are crazy liars. They "listen" to each other with a predisposition not to listen, which means they ultimately have little influence over each other.

Barrier 4: Being Right   Sometimes, we're tracking along just fine until we run headlong into our "wall of rightness." We get so busy arrogantly constructing our rebuttal that we don't hear anything else.

Getting out of your own way poses great difficulty here because a lot of the time people are just *wrong*. I can't be the only one who thinks this way! (If I am, I guess everyone else is wrong!) When someone's saying something I know to be way off the mark, I'm thinking to myself, "Man, this guy's wrong." How do you handle that situation? What do you do when somebody is that wrong? Do you look at this person and say, "Wrong!"? Or maybe use some sort of leadership hand motion as you say, "Wrong!"? Or do you get clever and say things like "I know you're intelligent; I just can't tell that by talking to you!"? Maybe you sarcastically point out, "You joined the company three days ago, and I've been here 25 years— but maybe I just don't know enough."

None of these are very endearing options.

In our interviews with the top 1 percent, we addressed this barrier, and we noticed that top performers consistently did one thing: In a face-to-face situation with someone who's dead wrong, they simply never said the word "wrong." Instead, they used speech and body language that communicated, "I disagree with you, but I'm willing to listen." They prompted the speaker for more information.

When you take that path, three things can happen. First, you might find out that you're much more in agreement than you previously thought, because you listened. Second, you might realize they are nuts, but now you know *why* they're nuts, because you listened. Or third, they might start to change their story to match yours in an effort to look right in front of you or their peers or whoever is involved.

My point is this, and it covers all four barriers: If you hope to take advantage of the power of listening, get out of your own way! Whatever your barriers to listening, work through them so that you can make good use of this first building block for establishing trust: People are most likely to bond with people who listen more than they talk.

Gaining Agreement

In the answers our top performers gave about success, we discovered an interesting theme. The top 1 percent did something different—something most people deem irrelevant: They sought agreement rather than persuasion.

The top 1 percent know that to take trust building from the listening stage to something that feels collaborative, you've got to find a point or a premise you can actually agree upon. It's hard to collaborate when your dealings with someone are contentious. And the top 1 percent realize that people are much more likely to agree with people who agree with them first. So, when people carry on about their problems, top performers don't blurt out "That's not a problem!" and immediately go into their solution, adopting a tone of "How could you not know this?" Instead, they say, "I agree that that's a problem." They might carry that thought a little further— "In fact, I can tell just by *looking* at you that you have a problem." (I wouldn't exactly say it that way, but you get my point.) Then they explain the solution in an understanding and informative way.

Just because you can solve a problem in your head in seven seconds doesn't mean that you should. It's amazing how being intelligent can cause you to say things that are incredibly stupid.

Most successful people intrinsically understand that agreement is the foundation of accountability. Agreeing with people causes them to agree with you more readily, and they become more receptive and accountable to what you say. So why is it so hard to do? Our desire to always be right (barrier four, discussed previously) is a big part of the problem. As we listen, we get so entrenched in our own rightness that we feel compelled to prove someone else's wrongness.

The top 1 percent work to overcome that compulsion, knowing that if they push on and address other topics they are likely to find some less objectionable points to agree upon. People in the top 1 percent naturally seek agreement from the people they interact with. What they do is not completely effortless; they constantly have to remember to subdue gut reactions like "you're wrong" or "you're dumber than a box of rocks." But their process (which we call the collaborative toolkit) never failed them in their quest for agreement:

- Ask—ask a question.
- Listen—listen specifically for something you can agree with.
- Agree—let them know how much you agree with them.
- Recommend—make a recommendation based on that point you agree on.

This process forces you to push past all the listening barriers described previously. It requires you to find a kernel of truth in anything anyone says. Honestly, even near-truths will do. Maybe 90 percent of what the other person feeds you is psychotic BS, but don't blow past the 10 percent that isn't. Listen for it and jump right on it: "You know what? That last thing you said—I think you hit the nail on the head. I agree with you, and here's how I can help you." If you can do this, you've made the other party feel heard; you've made the other party right; and you've made yourself caring, competent, and influential.

In business, people tend to hold their trust in tightly clenched fists. With your intentional effort to listen and gain agreement, you begin to pry those fingers away from the palm, loosen that grip—and trust begins to seep out.

Whenever you agree with people, you've created an alignment of values that makes them more receptive to seeing value in other ideas you introduce. They begin to believe you think alike and start to view you as more effective. They see you as a go-to person, someone to call in on a problem, and they begin to act as if they're fixing the situation themselves. Now that's trust. That's when you have influence.

The point is simple, and it is the second of the truths listed at the start of this chapter. People are most likely to agree with people who do not make them feel wrong. If you now focus on the third observation from our study, you'll have people fully opening up that fist for a handshake—a sure sign that they're willingly placing their well-guarded (and hard-earned!) trust in your hands. And that's a lot better than having that clenched fist hit you in the face.

Their Input in Your Solution: Brilliance!

To solidify their influence, top performers make a habit of letting people know how important their input was to solving their problem. That's the success factor behind the ask-listen-agree-recommend process. Ask-listen-agree-recommend yields effective results because people rarely object to their own ideas. We are narcissistic; the idea that sounds best to us is the one we were thinking of already. No idea looks better than *my* idea. So my idea coming from you is a *fantastic* idea. Whatever you just said that sounds like an idea I already had—that must be a *great* idea because it's living in my head, and you just said it.

So, when you find a point you agree on and then recommend a solution that incorporates that point, it's like the other person helped create the solution. After all, what comes out of someone else's mouth means a lot more to that person than what comes out of your mouth. People are tightly tied to their own ideas, and they love it when their input—not yours—solves the problem. If they see some aspect of themselves in what you have to offer, then what you have to offer carries more weight. In their eyes, you've proven yourself to be competent and compassionate and *nearly* as brilliant as they are. You've stacked those building blocks of trust to make a sturdy structure you can climb to achieve success—which sure beats falling off the big pile of #@%! you create when you try to be right all the time.

You've also realized the third truth of business we observed: People are most likely to value a solution they helped to create.

The Breakdown: Complexity Frequently Fails

Once you master these first three truths about business—the building blocks of trust—you can start to embrace the final three. Let's start with one that surprises anyone who has been taught that complexity indicates superiority. After all, the more complicated something is, the more effective it must be, right? But the truth is that successful people will abandon anything that's too complicated.

Do you think you may be hiding behind complexity? Some people feel they prove their intelligence by making things look complicated. I call it having difficulty with simplicity. If every time a solution comes your way you say, "It's not that simple," you might be operating under the protection of complexity. Of course, it's human nature to want to be seen as intelligent. And we think complexity not only demonstrates intelligence but value. After all, if others knew how easily we did some things or how easily we saw the solution, that knowledge might undermine our image! Better to be difficult and complex.

Yet actually the opposite is true: The more moving parts something has, the more likely it is to break down. It's the basics of mechanical engineering. You've got to keep things simple and clear. If you make things look too complex, people might question the process, poke holes in it, or deem it unimportant. We think we have to feed more complex information to our higher-ups so we can prove to them how smart and useful we are. But when CEOs get a memo with more than five bullet points on it, they ignore it or pass it off to someone at a lower level who can't really make the big decisions.

First-Level Lesson

We choose what makes us feel secure and abandon things that don't.

We might use scatter charts (charts that only people who lack clarity can read) and algebra to make a decision, but it's only because those things make us comfortable. They allow us to make the decision we want and feel like we made it based on facts. We have a tendency to choose what makes us comfortable, even if it is not the best idea or product. It's why some people hang on to the favorite comfy shirt they love so much, even though when they wear it in public people consistently hand them a dollar.

I'd like to think that because I'm a master communicator, I have this unbelievable relationship with my 13-year-old stepdaughter. I'd like to think we have a tight bond and that she talks to me about things she doesn't talk to her mother or father about. But the truth is she knows I'll buy her better stuff than anybody else will. When it comes down to it, she knows Garrison will spring the cash for things that mom and dad might question. And ultimately, she really knows I'm a one-rule parenting person: Nobody gets pregnant. I don't care what you do as long as there's no pregnancy involved. You can talk on the phone forever, go to late-night birthday parties, do all those things your mother thinks I shouldn't let you do—just don't get pregnant. You do your homework, you do this, that, and the other—the main thing is: Don't get pregnant.

Okay, maybe I shouldn't be proud of my one-rule parenting style, but it illustrates an important truth about complexity: You've got to keep your solution, process, or idea simple and clear.

Otherwise, you jeopardize your chances of quick acceptance. It's very difficult to be effective if you're going to make things complex. We run the risk of leaving open too many holes for questions we can't answer and too many opportunities to provide answers that seem like fluff rather than substance. That reminds me of my other simple rule: No substance abuse. The truth is that if you are not on drugs or pregnant, you've had a fairly successful teenage-girl day! This is simplicity at its finest.

Second-Level Lesson

People choose what makes them feel valuable.

It's difficult to decide that the thing you don't understand, the thing that intimidates you, is the right choice. No one ever says, "I know that this choice will make me appear useless to mankind, and I'm afraid the details are just way over my head, but I just have to go with my gut." What we really want long term are the things that boost our sense of self-worth. Sure, we want a lot of stuff that is bad for us (some of us never recover from those wants), but deep down we need our choices to make us feel like we are making a contribution to the world. Value is the foundation of comfort.

Simply Effective

I'll never forget a vivid example of the effectiveness of simplicity I came across a few years ago. I saw two financial advisors giving presentations on understanding your relationship to risk. One presenter had all kinds of PowerPoint slides and scatter charts. In fact, he actually seemed surprised by his own PowerPoint slides—as in

"Here's a slide that seems interesting." I don't think *he* knew what was on those slides. He was not very good and certainly not memorable, other than for his bumbling way of navigating around his own presentation. His message was lost on us.

On the other hand, the second advisor's presentation was simple. He stood up in front of us and said: "Here's what you need to know about how you personally feel about financial risk. You just have to ask yourself these three questions: Do you like traveling at 55 miles per hour? Do you prefer to go 75 miles per hour? Or do you want to go 100 miles per hour?

"At 55 miles an hour, you won't get caught for speeding, but you're not going to get anywhere very fast. Not much risk; not much reward. At 75 miles an hour, you can get somewhere pretty fast, but if you get caught speeding, you'll probably get a ticket that'll cost you some money. If you go 100 miles an hour, you can get there fast and be effective and maybe get rich by being the first to arrive, but you *will* pay if you get caught. So the question is: How fast do you want to go? Where is your level of risk? How afraid of going to jail are you?"

Simple points accompanied by clear illustrations that everyone in the audience could identify with. Afterwards, Mr. Scatter-Chart-Super-Slides was lost while this guy was a human client magnet with customers following him everywhere.

This all ties back to the Chapter 1 sidebar that reveals how 479 out of 500 CEOs we surveyed agreed that if you can't explain something very well, you don't have much value. An inability to explain something simply and concisely indicates that you don't understand your own information well enough, you don't have the communication skills you need, or you're not willing to take the time to create a simple explanation. (That is, you're not overly concerned with actually being good at what you do.)

In talking to these CEOs, I was shocked to learn that almost all of them had gotten rid of high-level employees who literally did not understand their own information well enough or who made things convoluted and complex. If you don't understand the information, it does not matter *how* simple you make it because you don't know what you're talking about! But these CEOs indicated that the more frequent problem was competent employees refusing to make their explanations simple. If these employees' explanations made things appear too simple, they thought it would look like they weren't working hard enough and weren't worth the money they were being paid because their work was too easy. Instead, these employees hid behind complexity right up to the point the CEO made the simple statement, "You're fired."

A Lesson from Addled Aunt Ethel

Even smart people struggle to state things clearly and simply. One year, my father and I went to visit my Aunt Ethel, who I always remembered as being pretty sharp. At the time Aunt Ethel was fairly old—somewhere between, say, 85 and death. We hadn't seen her in about 20 years. When we walked in her room, she looked at me and commented, "You look more like your daddy than your daddy looks like himself." And then she clarified. "Your daddy, who doesn't look like anybody now, did then. You know."

No, we don't know.

It doesn't matter how smart you are if nobody can understand you. It does not matter how results-oriented your complex process is if people have trouble sticking with it. Sometimes simple is more difficult than difficult, but the payoff is big in terms of getting people to track along with you.

And if you think that last statement surely proves my blood relation to Aunt Ethel, let me clarify. Making something sound simple often takes significant time and effort, but it's worth it. You'll find that if more people can understand it, more people will embrace it. If few people understand it, lots of people will reject it. That's the fourth simple truth of business: People are most likely to abandon a complex process, even if it works.

Clear, Simple, Comfortable Choice

In Chapter 1, I introduced the concept that people often refuse the best, opting instead for the most comfortable, the most familiar, or the simplest choice. More people read *USA Today* than the *New York Times* because it has color photos, plenty of pie charts, and fewer long words. Is it the better news source? No. The simpler source? Yes, by far! Simplicity sells.

This concept plays out in front of us during every presidential election in the United States, especially the 2004 race between incumbent President George W. Bush and Senator John Kerry, the Democratic challenger. The goal of any election is to get elected, not to prove who is more intelligent; you need to influence the voters.

When it came down to being influential, Kerry stood little chance of winning because he campaigned in compound sentences. His ideas and thoughts took time. Whether you agreed with those ideas or not, Kerry took forever to state them. It wasn't good for an immediate sound bite. Kerry said things like "I believe that this country can do something that it hasn't been able to achieve in a long time—it can achieve a level of greatness, achieve goodwill with other countries the world over. I believe that we can be the kind of America that the rest of the world will respect." Then, Bush would say, "I believe in America!" You can't compete with that. One of those sound bites will make the news and be easily understood by the voters; one won't. That's a simple case of using your intelligence against yourself. Kerry's media wounds were self-inflicted. Bush, on the other hand, was not held back by such handicaps.

Throughout history, presidential elections are full of examples like this. An unengaging candidate who can't speak clearly or debate well gets beaten by a charismatic opponent who communicates clearly. Elections are primarily popularity contests. Campaigning for presidential office has little to do with who will make the best president and everything to do with influence—a person's ability to explain things clearly, effectively, and with some charisma. You don't have to have a lot of charisma—you just need to have more than the other candidate.

This is why voters have selected some of the biggest losers for the Oval Office for reasons that had nothing to do with policy. (Ulysses S. Grant won mainly because he won the Civil War. He made a good general but was a horrible president who was, by some accounts, better at drinking than decision making.) Sometimes we elect presidents because they sound so different from the previous president (Ronald Reagan, for example). But there's one thing we won't do: We never, ever elect presidents who are less handsome, less charismatic, and less understandable than their opponents. Clarity carries more weight than intelligence when it comes to gaining support as a leader.

So while we would like to believe that the decisions we make always reflect the superior option, our research supports the opposite: If the best doesn't always win, surely it's not *us* but *everyone else* who's throwing their support behind the inferior-but-comfortable option. In corporate training sessions, I use the following lesson to shed some light on the truth about our tendencies.

The Plumber Exercise

A plumber pulls up to a customer's home in a dented truck. He comes to the door with his bad-plumber hair and a heavy tool belt weighing down those white plumber pants that will lead to the inevitable butt cleavage and says, "I'm here to fix the garbage disposal." The man lets him in.

The plumber asks, "Did you put anything weird in the disposal?"

"No," the customer replies.

The plumber starts pulling stuff out of the disposal and making comments: "You've got a pair of socks in here! Here's a beer bottle. Do you *know* the difference between a garbage can and a garbage disposal?"

The plumber fixes the disposal in record time but like most plumbers doesn't clean up after himself very well. As he leaves, he looks back at the customer and asks, "Are you going to put anything else weird in that garbage disposal?"

"No."

The plumber follows up with a phone call the next day: "Is that garbage disposal still working?"

"Yes."

"No can opener or anything stuck in there yet?"

"No."

"Great. Keep up the good work then."

After I present this story to a group, I then ask: With the service now complete, on a scale of one to five (with five meaning really good and one meaning really bad), how would you rate the plumber? I break them into groups to talk it over. They typically end up with high ratings, usually between four and five. We always have some group that comes up with a rating of 3.69; that's the IT team, apparently.

So, we get all these fantastic numbers—these are good numbers! The groups cite reasons such as these: "He followed up," "He fixed the problem in record time," and "He indicated what not to do." With all the positives weighed, the focus turns to negatives. What didn't you like? Responses range all over, but in general I hear comments to the effect that the plumber was kind of rude and not at all sympathetic, he was unpolished in appearance and attitude, and he didn't communicate sensitively enough.

Now, I tell the group to keep that plumber in the back of your mind while we talk about a new plumber in town. This plumber is really good-looking. In fact, he has a shiny new truck with a picture of himself on it! Someone you trust highly recommends him. This person told you, "For your next plumbing need, you should definitely use this plumber!"

Would you pick this plumber for your next plumbing need?

Typically, anywhere from 40 to 90 percent of the people in my sessions say they would. What just happened is an amazing thing. The first plumber was just rated with fours and fives and high threes—not a rating of two in the room! How could he be rated that high and lose between 40 and 90 percent of his business instantly to someone who has done nothing?

The people in my sessions marvel at this turn too. When I ask the groups what happened, they tend to respond, "I don't know." So I walk them through a pop culture example. I'll say, "What do Tonya Harding and the late Michael Jackson have in common?" Someone usually responds, "They both have suffered from a bad reputation. They both had fame that faded based on that reputation."

It's true. Michael Jackson's album *Thriller* ranks right up there with another of the bestselling albums of all time, Pink Floyd's *Dark Side of the Moon*—certain proof that the music-buying public is equally fond of dancing and smoking pot. But sales of *Thriller* dropped dramatically when the one-gloved King of Pop encountered some problems. (I'm not saying he was guilty of the formal complaints lodged against him. But I do think he was guilty of at least nine counts of being weird.) As Jackson has shown, one surefire way to restore the adulation of fans is to actually die. Jackson was a great talent who will be missed by many, but only time will tell if he is remembered more for his talent or for his odd behavior.

After a physical attack was made on rival figure skater Nancy Kerrigan, two-time Olympian Tonya Harding sank to a level of disrepute that now has her doing—what? Mud boxing? I'm not really sure *what* she's doing. And I'm not really sure what mud boxing is, but if you *are* mud boxing, let's just say that you are not at the pinnacle of your career. Harding's behavior sold out her skill, cheapened her accomplishments, and sucked all perceived value right out of her with the power of an industrial-grade Shop-Vac.

Most people recall their own reaction to Jackson's or Harding's fall from grace, which helps them understand the lesson's portability from pop culture to business culture: Your behavior can jeopardize others' appreciation of your skill, talent, or value.

The Lesson: Behavior Betrays Skill

I wish I could tell you that our interviews with the top 1 percent indicated that if you're talented enough, you can overcome almost anything. But our research didn't show that. Instead, our research showed that your behavior would betray your skill. If people don't like your behavior, they simply look for reasons not to trust you or agree with you.

What comes out of your mouth and how you conduct yourself create the perception around you, so you had better be aware of your behavior, even if you think it's justified. We cover this in greater detail in Chapter 7. For now, just keep in mind that if you don't focus your words and actions on making people feel valuable, you won't get much business from or have much influence over them.

Plumber No. 1 might argue that he had good reason to speak with contempt as he pulled socks and a beer bottle from the disposal. And we all agree he was an expert at repair. But his attitude, lackluster appearance (butt cleavage is rarely a crowd-pleaser), and careless cleanup lose him business as soon as some good-looking but relatively unproven competition comes to town. Plumber No. 1 might be the best in town, but lots of people in that town won't choose the best because a more comfortable option has presented itself.

The plumber is the epitome of our fifth truth about business: People don't often choose the best idea, the best products, or the best service. They choose what they are most comfortable with, whether it's the best or not.

The Importance of Feeling Important

In the coming chapters, I'll introduce you to two managers who achieved success by making others feel important. One of them got great results from his employees because he made them all feel as important as his own family. This enabled him to make difficult requests of his employees who would then work hard to please him for fear of letting "Dad" down. Another leader, not terribly innovative himself, regularly doled out recognition for his employees' innovations. His lavish praise of their achievements made them feel important and encouraged them to remain industrious.

These managers were the embodiment of the sixth, and final, truth about business that our research uncovered: People are most likely to follow leaders who make them feel important; those leaders are most likely to elicit the best performance. Let's get real—if your boss makes you feel useless, you simply figure out the least amount of work you can do without getting fired and then you hotly pursue your goal of mediocrity.

The top 1 percent understood that if people feel valuable, they're more dedicated. Their performance goes up. If you're not focused on making people feel valuable, you won't get much from the people around you. If you make them feel valuable, they work more safely and have fewer incidents on the job. If they feel less expendable on the job, they'll be more conscientious and more productive.

These findings mesh well with an idea from Marcus Buckingham and Curt Coffman in *First, Break All the Rules*: People don't work for companies; they work for their direct supervisors. The relationship they have with their direct supervisor is what their work life actually looks like. Nobody goes home and complains, "Man, the company as a whole is a problem." No, when they sound off, it sounds a little more like "Man, my boss Jeff is a *jerk!*"

So, while Plumber No. 1 might not qualify as a leader, he could learn a little something from this crucial observation: If he had made the customer feel important, he might get more loyalty from that customer. The customer might be more careful about the clothing items and household tools that find their way into the disposal. All right, so maybe that's bad for repeat business *but* when something does go wrong, the customer would be sure to call this plumber again. And that definitely is good for repeat business.

The Takeaway

Our research uncovered a heap of details—hundreds of them—that fed into our six observations about the truth of business. In reviewing these six points, you might sense a little redundancy—and you're right. This repetition, just like any example in this book, underscores the importance of and interrelationship between making people feel important and making them comfortable. Every one of the observations points back to the idea that we're creatures of comfort who like to be valued:

- Letting people talk and feel heard makes people feel comfortable and important.

- Agreeing with people validates their opinions, making them feel important and upping their comfort quotient with anything you subsequently suggest.
- Letting people's input show up in your solution makes them feel important and makes them immensely comfortable with you and your solution.
- Keeping your process or solution simple makes people comfortable and important because they can see themselves successfully implementing it.
- Having people be comfortable with what you have to offer reinforces your value, whether or not you're the best—it's all fine and dandy if your product, idea, or solution is the best, but you hedge your bets for success if you also make it something that most people will find familiar and in line with their preferences.
- Making people feel important makes them feel, well, important; most people are comfortable with that. Similarly, people who feel important tend to be comfortable with working harder and producing more for you.

These truths about the business culture provide you with great insight into how to position your advantage. What do you have to offer that can boost someone's value? What qualities about you can make someone comfortable? What aspects of your innovative solution can be made to resemble things that people are already comfortable with? If you can identify angles that help you apply our six observations to your advantage, you have what it takes to edge out the competition. Also, if you think this is all too simple and has no real value, then you might be too smart to be successful!

7

What Most People Will Not Do

From the outside in: looking deeply into
how others see you

WISDOM TELLS US, DON'T JUDGE A BOOK BY ITS COVER. BUT WE do. We won't bother to look at a book, much less read it, if we are not hooked or intrigued by the title and cover. If I walk by *Stuff That You Were Not Crazy About from Other Books You've Already Read and Didn't Like Very Much*, I'd be hard-pressed to add it to my reading list. But give me a book titled *How to Lose Weight: Eat Pizza and Sleep Late* and I'll at least skim the table of contents! And I think anyone seeing *How to Be Really Successful without Doing Anything* would probably pick it up and at least scan the first chapter (although technically that means they've done *something*).

Like it or not, we judge people by their covers too. This is especially true in business. Statistics show that 80 percent of impressions in business are formed in the first five minutes. Think about it. Do we eat food that looks rotten or smells and tastes bad? For most of us, the answer is a resounding no. When people call certain foods an "acquired taste," this just means that those foods taste horrible.

It also means that those people are just trying to sound impressive. If I think caviar tastes like low tide at the boat ramp, it doesn't matter how expensive it is. Now, I'm not equating you to caviar or some stinky, low-tide residue; I'm just saying that if people don't quickly take to you, it doesn't matter how much you have to offer them.

How others see and perceive us in those first few minutes of our meeting them has a direct effect on our ability to be successful. And we need to maintain that perception 100 percent of the time. This is the essential first step to realizing or creating your personal advantage. It's possible to rule the world (or at least start a cult) based on self-discovery and capitalizing on innate advantages. But knowing and *controlling* how others see us affects our ability to navigate the continual challenges of business.

For many of us, believing the perceptions we have of ourselves is the armor we wear to get through life. But often we are our own biggest problem. As we learned in Chapter 4, the top performers we surveyed knew how others perceived them and used that information to their *advantage*. Those who have the insight and strength to work past our basic natural resistance to admit our weaknesses and find a way to use them to their advantage are the ones heading to the top—not that this is easy for anyone to admit and talk about, even when they reach the top. Most people want us to notice their greatness, not their drawbacks.

Think you're really aware of how the world sees you? Ask yourself these questions:

- Do you think that what you see in the mirror is what others see?
- If you don't know, are you willing to get the honest answers that will tell you?
- Do you have the talent needed to help you reach your goals?

- Are you disappointed in what you discovered about yourself in the first three questions?
- Can you move past your disappointment and positively focus on moving forward?

If you answered no to any of the first three questions, you have your work cut out for you in this chapter. It's emotionally painful for a lot of people to get real about how they're probably viewed because of the self-esteem issues we all struggle with. If you answered no, you still do. Get over yourself! Again as we learned in Chapter 4, your ego can be an advantage but only if you understand consistently how you are perceived. Consider the story of Armando, who had already made a bad first impression but showed us how someone can take what could have been a permanent disadvantage and turn it into a formula for success.

Be and *Own* Who You Are

Armando was a wholesaler who was trying to establish himself with grocers across the country. But his thick Mexican accent made it difficult for him to communicate clearly in English. Frustrated, he realized that his ideas and products were being dismissed because of the way he spoke; people judged him by his "cover," his accent. Grocers saw him as a classless outsider and, regardless of what he had to offer, not what they wanted in a partner.

Was this fair? Of course not, but remember what this book has been saying: Life and business are always unfair. Call it bigotry or even stupidity on the part of the grocers, and you'd be right. Armando had two choices: bang his head against the wall for the rest of his life or honestly understand how other people saw him and use this information to his advantage.

"I had to take a look at who I was," Armando explained. "If I told grocery store owners that I was an expert in Cornish game hens, they wouldn't listen; they had plenty of other Cornish game hen wholesalers who didn't have a thick accent. But when I told them I was an expert in Hispanic foods and knew what this community would buy, suddenly they loved talking to me. There was no way a Caucasian could compete with a Hispanic guy selling Hispanic foods with distributor connections who all speak Spanish."

Sometimes we have to use other people's prejudices against them to level the playing field. Armando was getting ready to go from being the victim of an unfair situation to the victor of an unfair fight.

He knew that Hispanics were traditionally known to walk through grocery stores and not purchase much. Grocers thought it was just a lack of money, but they knew it was a growing market. Perceived now as a representative of this market, Armando showed them how their shelves lacked products Hispanics needed to cook. He knew that an immigrant housewife of Mexican descent was not going to make dinner with the stuff she saw in their stores. Her experience would be something like mine when I was in Indonesia and went to the market looking for ham. What they showed me did not seem, for lack of a better description, piglike. But this woman was going to cook. Contrary to trends that showed more people cooking less and eating out more (leaving grocers scrambling for precooked meals to offer), Armando knew that many Hispanics continued to cook at home out of tradition. And he not only knew what they were looking for, but he knew where to get it.

Armando had stacked the deck in his favor. He looked and sounded like what he was selling access to, and the grocers were convinced he knew what would attract people to their stores. He knew the other grocers figured his "Mexican-ness" would position him to bring in the business. Instead of fighting the impression he made, he used it to his advantage and became a pioneer in grocers' efforts to sell to the nation's Hispanic population.

In short, Armando had become exactly what these grocers perceived him as and used it to his advantage. He might have lost his first unfair fight, but he did what needed to be done to set up the next one and win. So it stands to reason: Understanding that people's perception of you is often reality can help you avoid losing in the first place. It also tells us that being Caucasian and well positioned does not make you exempt from stupidity.

Maybe those grocers immediately took note of Armando's ethnicity, but the first thing I noticed when I met Armando was his mink bomber jacket. "That is like nothing I have ever seen," I said. He looked like a bear from a very expensive flight school. When I asked where he got that jacket, he told me he paid $25,000 to have it custom made. "Why would you do that?" I asked. He said, "Because I can."

Had Armando ignored the perception that most people had of him, he could have been the most unsuccessful wholesaler of Cornish hens in his market. But because he revised his approach and identity to match what others saw, he's now wildly successful in a booming niche market and has the mink coat to prove it.

Contrast Armando's story with this one from a top performer named Tom. Tom started out by building industrial instrumentation products in his garage and grew his business to compete at a global level. Open, honest, and straightforward, this guy made no bones about his ego and was not afraid to get real about his shortcomings, and he helped me understand how successful people use their shortcomings to be successful from the start.

Tom knew that his competition in industrial instrumentation focused on being experts in all the industry's applications. As he prepared to launch his career, he was preparing to come off as the expert too, but preliminary research had convinced him that his lack of an engineering degree combined with his unscientific, conversational style undermined his credibility. Then his wife pointed out to him that he had the ability to deliver "digs" at people without having anyone perceive them as negative. She told me, "He would say things at the dinner table that really offended me but no one *else* seemed to think they were offensive." (Of course, she was his ex-wife at the time I interviewed her.)

Tom knew she was right; he also knew he couldn't compete as an expert so he didn't. Instead, he used his conversation skills and what he understood about his own ego to make customers want him. In his regular-guy, nonscientific way, he would say to customers, "You know more about your application than anyone else does, and don't let anyone tell you differently." Thus, Tom planted seeds of doubt about competitors without ever mentioning their flaws or saying he was superior. In fact, he had made his clients feel superior to all of them! This guy has a talent for knocking the competition without making anyone (including himself) actually look bad.

Remember what we learned in Chapter 6: What comes out of someone's mouth when you are trying to get buy-in on an idea means more to that person than whatever comes out of your mouth. People like things that sound like what they were already thinking: "Wow, what you just said sounds like what I was just thinking! My idea sounds fantastic coming from you! I think we should do that." It seems that people are narcissistic even when seeking an outside opinion.

So Tom had connected to his clients' ego. He would then say things like "X Company is a big company, and they do a fine job but they have 3,000 accounts like yours. I have five, so frankly you mean a lot more to my company, and I am able to give you a much deeper level of attention. Nothing against them; I'm sure they would care more about you if they actually knew who you were."

Having used his regular-guy approach to establish trust, he made sure he gave honest answers to questions his prospective clients had (and sometimes he even planted pivotal questions so he could deliver honest answers). If they asked how well his product really worked, he'd say, "It worked great at the trade show in Chicago but not so well at the plant. It'll give you gas-gage accuracy—as in, you'll know when you're full and you'll know when you're empty, but along the way I can't guarantee a 357.5 liter reading. Instead you can just say you have about a quarter-tank left." I'm not sure what that means, but it sure sounds honest.

If they asked about the competition's claims to accuracy, he'd say, "I guess they couldn't say it if it *wasn't* true. It's just that in the 150 plant locations I've visited, the people who install and maintain the equipment—the ones who have nothing to gain by being dishonest—have never seen the kind of accuracy advertised. [Insert short pause and a head tilt.] That doesn't mean that out there somewhere someone isn't getting better results, though." In the words of my 13-year-old, "This dude is spooky-good."

Tom had them. They believed him. "I'm sure they mean well" was an extraordinarily effective nail in the competition's coffin. A few years later when his competitors wanted to buy him out, he used that same directness to tell them that he was very flattered that they considered him competitive but he was confident that what it would take to buy him out was more than even their "giant company" could afford. He told them that he was sure they had the ability to raise a lot of money and that he wasn't insulted by their offer, but since he loved what he was doing and since he was looking to expand globally to help customers get a realistic view of the solutions available, their offer was just nowhere close to enough. The competitors quickly doubled their offer.

The lesson is clear: Tom was willing to listen to what people said and take an honest look at how he was perceived, and then he *owned* it. He was not necessarily proud of his style—who wants to admit their disadvantage is their key to success? Tom admitted he had unsuccessfully tried to change it on many occasions. But nothing he did was unscrupulous or illegal, and he had made peace with it (even if his wife didn't).

So what if Tom would never be the expert who could compete with the established, 100-year-old companies with their parade of geniuses? Those people didn't have the business. He did. Let the scientists have their names on their lab coats; he had his name on the door. And he kept it there by always being the regular guy who was concerned about how his customers would be treated by the "big dogs." He told them the facts. He was on *their* side. The advantage of not being the most knowledgeable person in his industry is that he doesn't know enough to be condescending. For example, you'd never hear him say something like "This may be a bit complicated, but I'll try to use layman's terms." All Tom *had* were layman's terms.

Tom and Armando accepted and embraced who they were and used it to their advantage. They, like so many in the top 1 percent, were satisfied with who they were, how they were perceived, and the advantage that gave them. Most of us are not satisfied with who we are. We expect much more of ourselves, but too often we expect the *wrong* things for who we are. Think about how others see you. It's a difficult and often painful discovery, but in business it is essential to your success. Own it.

Acceptance is not easy, but neither is being wrong about who you are. You might need to adjust your environment to you, not the other way around. It's like the guy in the peach-colored leisure suit and unstable hairpiece (which looks like a large rodent died on his head) who believes he's the coolest thing in town. In reality, if he were at a '70s retro party, he would be.

Why Getting Real Does Not Mean Getting Happy

Our research, the Gallup Institute research cited in *First, Break All the Rules*, and most mental health professionals agree: Getting real about your behavior and how it affects others is what the most successful and well-adjusted people on the planet have in common. I'm not talking about being happy. During our research, we met as many successful people who were not happy as we did unsuccessful people who were unhappy. You don't have to like yourself to be successful. You can be a jerk, have low self-esteem, and *know it*, and *still* have an advantage over the jerks with low self-esteem who don't know it.

Happiness seems to be a by-product of two things: Treating people well and general lack of information. Knowing a lot has the potential to lead to unhappiness. Everyone these days wants knowledge, right? Yet when the things we discover are difficult or dangerous, it negatively affects our happiness.

Happiness and unhappiness with life are important issues to ponder, but I want to make one thing perfectly clear: This book is absolutely not about being happy. I would really like it if everyone could find happiness. But this book is about what the most successful people have in common, and the bottom line is that there are a lot of successful people who are happy and about just as many who are not. Happiness doesn't seem to be a necessary product of success. Go to a bus station, and you will find happy people and miserable people. Go to a country club, and you'll find the same. Simply put, money does not buy happiness, and poverty does not guarantee misery. However, money and poverty do guarantee other things in our society. Really poor people are never reported as missing on the national news, and really rich people never get the death penalty for murder. So money will buy you something—just not rainbows and unicorns!

But I have noticed that the most successful people I've met enjoy the actual process that it took to be successful. I could not find many people at the top of their game who really hated what they were doing.

Contrary to popular belief, it is possible to do a job well that you don't like. And some people hate what they do and still do pretty well—big houses, big cars, money in the bank—but none of them have what it takes to reach the top. Those people seem to possess a projectile misery that is not fun to be exposed to. They may be able to do anything while hating it, but they are very hard to work with and their toxic energy will make you want to shoot yourself! Misery does not always love company, but it does love to express itself to those of us who seem to be enjoying our success.

Even though this book is not about finding happiness, I do believe that if you honestly look at yourself and how others see you and make choices that will develop your personal advantage, you will feel a sense of satisfaction from knowing that you're using your skills and making your best effort. You will feel a sense of completeness and a bit better than when you started. So perhaps happiness is created by the effort expended rather than being the ultimate outcome that results from that expended effort. It's food for thought that might be slightly hard to swallow right now.

This was never clearer to me than when I grew my own company to a size that I was unqualified to run. I wanted to believe that I could control my own company's day-to-day operations, but I was failing and standing in the way of my own success. I didn't have the organizational skills to operate my own organization! I also had some small problems with accounting—namely, math, which is just slightly important. I had to accept that I was unqualified to run this company that I had started. I had to actually coin a phrase for myself: *dinosaur founder*—a person who creates something and then works his way toward extinction. Talk about a bitter pill to swallow! So I faced the fact that I had been the biggest hindrance my company had. I hired someone smarter than I am, and to my disgust, things got a lot better.

Later in this annoyingly painful journey to embrace my limitations and how I am perceived, I asked someone if he thought I was passive-aggressive. He answered, "No, you are *aggressive*-aggressive!" While I still feel the sting of that insult (this happened in 2001!), I also learned that it's easy for me to dominate conversations. I'm like concentrated laundry detergent—a little of me goes a long way!

I have a tendency to make light of almost everything and run the risk of offending people with some of the information that I have gathered and passed along. But I have learned that my style, if monitored carefully, gives me an advantage. That's why you are still here reading. Those who have quit reading are like the Amish. We can say what we want about them because they will never find out! Please note: If you *are* Amish and you are reading this book, I know that you probably have a 1972 Buick that you keep hidden in town.

The bottom line is a truth that I learned the top 1 percent understand: Getting real about how you come across to other people is not a journey everyone wants to make, and it is not for the faint of heart.

Perception Is Reality

You must be willing to get real about how you are viewed by others, accept how they see you, and get past how you *want* them to see you. Perhaps some people can effectively change the way others perceive them, but it is much easier, much more realistic and effective, to understand how you are viewed and find a way to make it work for you. We have to understand what other people see when they see us.

Think about actors. Actors can never be successful unless they are believable in the roles they are cast for. TV shows about gorgeous people who can't seem to get asked out on a date really don't connect with viewers. I just saw a movie in which Jennifer Aniston's character got dumped by a guy who in real life could have never gotten past Aniston's security people because he is too goofy to even get an autograph. If we are willing to get real about how we appear to others, we can take advantage of an image that exists rather than one that needs to be created. So when Coach was teaching your health class in high school (honestly, was there anyone less healthy than Coach?), you were not inspired to catch the healthy eating bug. It's like being faced with a chubby doctor who smells like cigarettes—that person just does not have a lot of credible influence.

I remember watching some old movie where the producers had cast some extraordinarily blue-eyed, blond-haired actor as Poncho Villa. There was just no way to suspend the disbelief! Perhaps they thought he was such a big star that he would draw the audience despite completely not fitting the part. Even in Hollywood, most people just have to fit the part. You might think you're the Brad Pitt type, but the world looks at you as Paul Giamatti. Brad Pitt, no matter how good he is, could never pull off the Paul Giamatti roles. If you look like Paul Giamatti and you go after a bunch of Paul Giamatti roles, then you're much more likely to be successful. If you don't know who Paul Giamatti is, you've made my point even stronger.

I met a top-performing sales guy who was really scary looking (think Lurch from *The Addams Family*). I thought, "Who would buy from this guy?" Then I found out that he sold embalming fluid and other death products. I somehow got the feeling that he really knew what dead people needed! He suddenly looked very credible in his role.

One time I auditioned for a movie, and I was cast in the part of a lecherous drunk. (This concerned me greatly; I mean, what does *this* say about me?) After I auditioned, I sat in a room filled with guys who looked and acted a lot like, well, me. It was actually kind of creepy. Anyway, I had the opportunity to talk with some of these other men before we knew who had gotten the role. One guy told me that the casting people told him he revealed a natural friendliness that was not what they were looking for in the character. When I learned that I got the role, I had to understand that I apparently was not perceived as naturally friendly. Apparently I was more naturally lecherous and drunklike.

The key to success is getting the right person in the right role. Many notable self-help business books—including *Good to Great* and *First, Break All the Rules*—tell you this: Put the right people in the right roles. That applies to you too. You have to learn to put yourself in the right role based on how you're perceived. We can't do just anything we set our minds to. In fact, research and evidence suggest that if you embrace that kind of thinking, there may actually be something *wrong* with your mind. I could never be an Olympic track star because I'm old and slow, not because I don't have the right attitude.

Chapter 9 shows you how to act and adapt in this role to create opportunity. For now, think back to our discussions in Chapter 4 about using your disadvantage to your advantage. For example, you think you're brilliant. Okay, you *know* you're brilliant. Then, you should also know that brilliance is not really a transferable commodity. You would be better served helping people develop their own brilliance—even if that means undercutting yours. If you admit your imperfections and talk about your own flaws and faults, you help others realize that everyone has challenges.

One thing I have learned about myself is that I can come across as really confident—so confident, in fact, that some view it as arrogance. Too much confidence can scare people away. So I really have to work on tempering myself, especially when presenting in front of a group that is looking for motivation and going through difficult times. I've got to make sure these people know I'm with them by opening up to them and showing them that I have problems too. If I don't humanize myself and talk about my problems—if I'm always the hero of my own story—I will come across as arrogant.

Confidence can kill if that confidence is perceived as arrogance. (You can add dramatic to my list of endearing qualities.) So what if I *know* that my ideas are pretty good, my research is pretty solid, and I believe those ideas and research are better than the next person's? That may be true or it may be my own ego talking (or a combination of the two). But my ability to be human—to say things and be honest about my own faults and myself first—is more powerful. As a result, I sometimes get the job not because I know more than my competition but because my delivery was funnier, clearer, more human, and more *connected* with the person looking to hire me.

Solutions: Solicit, Self-Scan—Whatever It Takes

While some people intuitively know how others perceive them, most of us paint a more flattering portrait of ourselves than other people see. Even a subtle difference in those renderings might dictate a change in approach. If I think I'm the picture of confidence but others consider me arrogant, the characteristic that I think helps seal the deal is the very thing that kills it. Hence the change in tactics I described on the previous page. Now I let people know that I'm just as flawed as anyone else and probably more inclined to laugh about and learn from my mistakes.

Can you see the importance of turning the bright interrogation lights on yourself? You need to separate that idealistic perception of yourself from the you that other people see. Are you up to this kind of self-scrutiny? If you don't think you can be that honest with yourself, it's all right. In this self-discovery process, soliciting is encouraged! Enlist a good friend who knows you well and whom you've always considered very perceptive. Bluntness is a desirable quality in this friend. So is bigness. If this friend tells you something you don't like hearing, you'll think twice before you pick a fight. (Flashback to Chapter 4: size matters.)

Your assignment, on your own or with your big blunt friend, is to scan your advantage possibilities. What do people notice most about you? Are you tall or big or cocky or kind or shy or fun to be with? Do you talk a lot? Are you a good listener? Are you obnoxious? Are you honest to a fault (which can sometimes *seem* obnoxious)? Are you friendly and approachable? Let's look at a few examples of how the possibilities can be parlayed into advantages.

Assessment: Your friend tells you that you seem shy but friendly.

Advantage: People are not threatened by you. You can be aggressive without stepping on toes.

Assessment: You're candid and forthright; you don't compromise integrity.

Advantage: In today's corporate world, suck-ups are everywhere. People in power often expect it but don't respect it. Play your strengths to audiences that seek candor and integrity. These qualities are what people or corporations seek when they're in dire trouble. On the brink of a disaster that can be averted, don't delude me with niceties or false optimism. Don't blow sunshine in dark crevices without offering honest evaluation and practical advice. Shoot straight, nail the problem, save the situation, be the hero. Your skills are in demand.

Assessment: You're so good-looking (or bad-looking!) that people stare.

Advantage: You attract attention and have a captive audience. (It's hard to escape ugly.) Capitalize on it! Give them something to tune in to. Engage them in conversation and ask plenty of questions so they're forced to respond rather than just gawk. This way, they won't write you off as unapproachable or dismiss you as little more than an objet d'art (or objet d'saster).

Assessment: Your laserlike focus intimidates people.

Advantage: You are seen as dedicated and powerful. You are able to convince others that what you are focused on has great value. You can lead people to see the vision you want them to embrace.

Be Responsible and Accountable

Despite learning that it's easier and more effective to accept how others perceive you, maybe you insist on changing everyone's view to agree with yours. (I bet your big blunt friend pointed out your stubbornness but you refused to acknowledge it.) To control how others perceive you, taking responsibility and being accountable at all times is essential. Nearly all of the top 1 percent we surveyed were willing to say something like, "Most of my problems are of my own making. It is my fault. If I hired this guy and he did all these terrible things that ruined my company, then maybe I don't hire well."

Even if there was some blame, ultimately these top performers saw things as their responsibility and accepted it. Even if you've been blamed for things that aren't your fault, you need to try to rein in your righteous desire to blame if you hope to achieve success. That's because blame—always pointing fingers at someone or something else—is one of the few disadvantages that offers little advantage. Blame conveniently allows us to avoid the burden of responsibility. It's a reflex action that deflects the judgment of others. "If I blame you well enough, they might not come after me." Blame is like the story where two friends are being chased by a bear. You don't have to outrun the bear, just your friend.

Blame is a real stumbling block to success. And when it comes to holding people accountable, blaming others just won't work. The truth about blame is that the person who blames the most is often seen as the person at fault because he or she is doing the blaming and others think that this person is trying to deflect the blame. We think we can blame people and somehow that will bring us results, but people will find a way to deflect the blame. (Sure, I have been accused of being the blamer, but my accusers have it all wrong!)

I call this syndrome *blame distribution*. It's when someone starts blaming, and the blame starts revolving. And once this vicious cycle happens, nothing gets done. Suppose I'm the leader of a team of people and I walk into a meeting and address the team like this: "Look, last month didn't go very well. As a matter of fact, it was terrible! Just horrible! Worst month we ever had! I'd like everybody to go around the room and talk about what you did that contributed to the dismal outcome and how you can do better." The room is silent as a tomb. This is how leaders who are *not* successful attempt to hold people accountable.

The way top performers make people accountable is by holding themselves accountable. Most people can't or won't do that. Ever! I couldn't do it until I was in my forties. My ego and my fear of having my employees view me as the problem stood in my way of changing. But it works. It works every single time when used sincerely (remember the "love" from Chapter 5).

Here's how a top performer does it: "Hey, let's talk about what happened last month. Last month was bad, the worst month in the history of the company. I'd like to start off and talk about my role as a leader and what I could have done differently. I could have had an extra meeting; maybe the memos could have been a bit clearer. So another meeting and clearer communication are things I could have done differently. Let's go around the room and talk about what we think we can do differently next time." Now I've made everyone accountable—including myself—and I've done it in a nonthreatening way. Everyone's willing to become accountable because it's totally uncool *not* to be accountable. I have created a culture of accountability.

This approach also extends to *not* blaming your boss in the same breath. If you've got some news to pass on and you gather your team, don't say something like this: "Everybody, look, we've got this new program coming down. It's a new way of doing things. Personally, I admit I think it's stupid and a terrible idea, but we've got to do it anyway."

First of all, you just threw your boss under the bus. Then you basically just told your employees that you have no authority, and you are a helpless victim of the leadership. How does it feel to be a spineless jellyfish lying belly up on the beach with the sea gulls hovering above? Jellyfish management: the process by which a leader proves he or she has no backbone; this leader will sting when attacked but appears squishy under pressure.

Bonding is not the same as blaming. We want to build a relationship with people, but we can do harm when we jump in the lifeboat with them and blame the captain for sinking the ship. Successful leaders take the initiative to say, "Look, we've got some stuff coming down from upstairs. It's going to be different, and we are going to have to make some adjustments. But I guarantee that, as a team, we can make things happen. Some of this stuff we might not understand or like, but it is our job to make this thing work, and we will." The job of a leader is to lead with confidence even when the direction does not naturally instill it.

Even more important, don't shift the blame to your boss in front of your boss. The outcome is rarely good. No matter how stupid you think he or she is, this bears repeating: Your boss is just smart enough to be *your* boss.

Our research showed a huge advantage in top performers who were willing to take responsibility by not blaming others. They had learned to hold themselves accountable for the role they played in their own problems. As one respondent told us, "I realized that my problem in front of customers was that I was just too intense. I am naturally a tense person, and in front of customers it would come off as tense and concerned. That made them nervous and did not inspire any confidence. I realized that the best thing I could do for my company was to get the hell away from my customers!"

This top performer realized that customers and employees had been afraid to tell him this until he had a meeting with one customer who employed someone he had known since high school. After the meeting, this high school friend told him, "Look, whatever you are doing in that meeting is not working. You're antsy, you're nervous, and you talk about things in a tense and pressured way. The people you brought with you are *really* good. Why don't you just let *them* talk? Frankly, you don't even need to be in the room!"

This was the best feedback he had ever gotten on how he was being perceived, and he held himself accountable for every bit of it. He immediately started to get away from being the person who dealt directly with the customers, and his business improved.

Be Unemotional

How people feel and react to the events in the day-to-day also gets in the way of their success. Top performers are not machines, but they can almost always handle their emotions, avoid outbursts, and exhibit emotional stability at the appropriate times (especially when others cannot).

I'm a pretty emotional person, but after I have an emotional situation, I am able to get back on track and center myself. Too many people cannot. Each emotional situation leads to more emotional situations throughout the day, week, and month. This constant up-and-down makes it nearly impossible to be successful. The top 1 percent understand this. They are able to control their emotions by identifying and understanding them. They can admit that "right now how I'm feeling is bad and ridiculous, but I won't feel this way in an hour. I won't feel this way tomorrow. I won't feel this way next week." They get perspective quickly and then take smart actions based on knowledge rather than make rash decisions clouded by emotions.

Being unemotional does not mean being heartless or thoughtless or cold. It means being perceived as able to control your emotions—using them when needed and controlling them when necessary. What do you look for when hiring, say, a receptionist to represent your company? Someone who's educated, polite, well-spoken, friendly? Maybe, but you are really looking for somebody who has a lot of good days in a row, doesn't freak out, and stays on their medication. Be honest—given a choice, we usually prefer limited drama. The best receptionist has emotional stability and doesn't scare people off.

Think about people who dabble in stocks: Most buy high and sell low in reaction to how they feel. They act in their panic, dumping stocks during a decline and buying again only after the market rises enough to move their emotions from reserved optimism to near euphoria. Few will ever make any money with this strategy because they are acting on fear, not on actual information. They say, "I realize I feel this way because I'm panicked, not because I'm basing my decisions on logic or probability."

In fact, we talked to one industry leader who unemotionally used his ability to *generate* emotions to his advantage. His employees all told us he was very supportive. They said he frequently used the word *love*, as in "You know I love you guys." This supportive and caring approach made the most talented people in the company want to work for him. At the time, the company had suffered through some really bad management, and people were trying to find a way to get out from under their current managers to work for this guy. His people told us that he behaved like a kind, caring, consoling father—the father nobody ever really has. One person said, "He was the kind of guy who, when things were going badly, would come to your office and pretty much cry with you."

When we interviewed him, we learned that he was quite aware of the feelings that people had for him. After all, he created them. Like so many top performers, he did not come across as remarkably impressive. He wasn't the magical, wonderful leader we expected after hearing the employees' praises. But he knew what his personal advantage was: His success came from making those employees feel the kindness and support he showed his coworkers. He was caring but, at the same time, quite calculating. He knew that people really believed that he cared, and he used it to great advantage. He was sincere and possessed the triple threat of influence: He was caring, calculated, and kind.

This person knew how much goodwill he had and how much people cared about him, and he used that knowledge to motivate his people to get things done and hold them accountable. He would say, "You know I care about you, and I was there through all the problems you've had. But I *have* to have this, I have to have it *this* way, and I have to have it *right* now. If there were any other way to do it, I would. If there were a way to get you out of it, I would. But I can't." Because he was perceived as caring, this came across as motivating, and he didn't get a lot of excuses or blame from people.

The bottom line is that this guy, like so many top performers, not only knew the power of controlling his emotions but also understood their power and then used others' perception of him as an emotional person to his advantage. His employees saw him as someone who cared about them as if they were his family.

The punch line is that this guy eventually ended up in jail. The friendly, kind, compassionate manager ended up in some trouble with something related to income tax, though no one would tell us exactly. He might have had another business on the side and evaded taxes. The offense wasn't clear—except that it had nothing to do with the company at which we interviewed him—but it happened, and he went to jail for about three months. After he got out of jail, the guy was still so extraordinarily well liked that the company welcomed him back like it was no big deal.

He once told me, "If I had someone who I knew felt about me the way I feel about my employees, this person would have great influence over me. So I know how influential I am." Wow. He may have been a criminal, but he sure knew himself. I guess he knew he was a caring criminal! It reminds me of a story I heard years ago about a guy who robbed a bank and asked the teller if she would lose her job for cooperating with him. She said she might, so he told her that he would yell and act scary so she would look forced to comply. Much like the caring manager I interviewed, this reasonable robber understood the power of being yourself.

My point is this: Sometimes *who* you are matters less than *knowing* who you are. To get the advantage, you don't have to be the greatest person in the world who possesses the most skills. If you know who you are, you can probably use that to your advantage no matter what.

8

Summoning the Willingness

How to cross the line from knowledge
to implementation

YOU HAVE COME FAR IN CREATING THE GROUNDWORK FOR YOUR
personal advantage. Now you need to be willing to use it. Being
aware of what sets you apart and actually *acting* on that awareness
seems to be hard for some people. It's time to follow through! Knowing what you are supposed to do and not doing it can make you feel
slightly depressed, so if you're reaching for your meds right about
now, you are definitely using this book correctly.

Start by putting your hard work into perspective. By now,
you've spent hours reading this book, and you've identified the
unique characteristics of your personal advantage. That advantage
isn't much of an advantage if you never put it into play. Why would
you work so hard to achieve so little?

Maybe you're an avid reader. Maybe you have no life (the combination of these two things is not uncommon). Somehow, I don't buy either scenario. You have come this far on desire and knowledge; the next step takes faith. Don't hesitate. All you have to lose is the opportunity to win. All you have to find is the willingness to act.

We constantly find ourselves in situations in which we dream of some type of advantage. You're standing in line in the grocery store with just a few items and little time to spare. Up ahead is an elderly woman moving at the speed of smell, her cart full of yogurt and cat food, obviously an overregulated woman with a pampered feline that, by the looks of things, eats from a crystal goblet. "Unbelievable!" you think. What you wish for next is that the grocery clerk will interrupt and say, "Excuse me, cat lady. Would you please let the gentleman behind you with Grape-Nuts, a newspaper, and a *life* get ahead of you?"

Put simply, we desire advantages all the time. We just would like them created *for* us. Identifying your personal advantage will get you nowhere if you are not prepared to act when the opportunity arises and *use* your advantage to create or expand on opportunities. Given the chance, my 40-plus-year-old legs can still beat that low-and-slow cat lady's cart to the line.

But suppose the thought of outsprinting cat lady makes me start feeling manipulative or opens up a space for misgivings of unfairness to creep in. I know my advantage but hesitate to use it. What does this say about me? Well, for starters, my desire to beat an elderly woman in a race is a clear sign that I might have suppressed some anger over my inability to take action. It also indicates that I might be kind of a jerk! But when you know you have an advantage and you consistently talk yourself out of acting on it, your emotions can come out in strange (and disturbing) ways.

Don't Just "Talk" It; "Walk" It

Have you ever heard someone say, "They can talk the talk, but they can't walk the walk"? The truth is that "talking the talk" is one skill, while "walking the walk" is another. Personally, I am good at walking the walk but much better at talking the talk. I am the living embodiment of the expression, "People teach best what they are trying to learn." I teach what I need to remind myself to do and what I'm striving to perfect. That's why I've written a book!

In fact, our research showed that people who are truly able to walk the walk are not necessarily skilled at talking the talk. How many times has the top salesperson become the top sales manager? More often than not, he doesn't succeed in management because he is a sales whiz with a narrow focus on his own sales advantage and lacks the skills or experience to understand the broad knowledge that a manager needs to succeed. How many top-10 athletes become top-10 coaches? None. And if a financial advisor is so great at making money, why does she always need other people's money to manage? Two different advantages are required in those positions, and even top performers don't have both. But they know what they have and hire others to do what they cannot.

A curmudgeonly 80-year-old businessman who had decades of success in his field once shared this piece of wisdom with me: "God does not pass out ham sandwiches at noon." Initially, I assumed that this was some kind of lunch prayer offered up by the senile. The guy then explained to me that this was his way of saying that life seems to give you very little if you appear constantly in need and quite a bit if you do not. He felt that there were a lot of people who wanted to be successful and have the things they desired very badly, but they didn't seem to want them *enough* to do what was necessary to get them. So they spent their lives wishing that what they needed would drop into their laps and criticizing people who were willing to take the action necessary to get the ham sandwich.

First-Level Lesson

Overcoming unwillingness requires taking stock of the discomfort of where you are.

When the fear or discomfort of what you're going through becomes greater than the fear of change, you change. (Did Carl Jung say that? Either he or some other dead, smart guy did.) People who are uncomfortable—whether they're in pain or afraid or they feel like they just can't tolerate their existence the way things are—are motivated to change. Some people never reach this level of fear or discomfort; they never reach this intolerance of their situation. Therefore, they have no great motivation to overcome their unwillingness. Personally, I believe that my own lack of tolerance for certain situations has helped me to achieve what I have. Someone once saw me drinking rice milk and commented, "Oh, are you lactose intolerant?" I said, "No, I'm just intolerant in general." So far, it has served me well by allowing me to see that if I dislike my situation strongly enough, I'll take actions—even actions that I'm not all that excited about taking—to move me out of that situation. As politically incorrect as it sounds, the key to overcoming unwillingness is a lack of tolerance.

I've observed something similar: People don't always do what they *need* to do, but they will do what they *want* to do. For example, I *need* to get more sleep, but I *want* to drink more espresso. The result is that I am sitting on a plane after rushing through traffic (the line at Starbucks slowed me down just a tad), jacked up on caffeine, and making a very convincing argument to my seatmate that sleep is overrated and that science can't prove it isn't, while he slowly backs away and molds himself into the shape of the window.

You can say that you *need* to make money. But can you find a want in that need to catapult you to success? The top performers we spoke to know that wishing and wanting won't get them where they need to go. What *will* get them there—what will compel them to implement their personal advantage—follows.

Confidence?

I've heard so many people say, "I need to be more assertive, but I want to curl up and hide." So why do you feel the need to be more assertive? What is it about assertiveness that you really want? (Don't say success.) Will your assertiveness allow you to be viewed as someone who is competent? Do you have the willingness to project that confidence? I say *project* because it is not as much about whether you are confident as it is that you *appear* to be confident. As we learned in the previous chapter, knowing how people perceive you is the first step. But then you need to capitalize on that perception and implement it as an advantage.

Many in our top 1 percent admitted that it was essential to appear confident at crucial times—suppressing any sense of doubt or fear. One of the top performers I interviewed told me that his confidence was often temporary; he kept his fear at bay until he achieved his aim and then retreated to the safety of his office.

"So you go back to your office, curl up in a fetal position, and cry?" I asked.

"Actually," he replied, "I sit at my desk and stare at the awards hung on the walls, wondering how it's possible that, with all my fears, I can be so successful. And I wasn't crying. I just had something in my eye." Never think people at the top don't know how to fake it until they make it.

In more than a decade of research and in my own experience, I believe that heroes and cowards feel the same fear. We touched on this at the end of Chapter 2: We all want to be the hero of the story. And we are often perceived that way, regardless of intent, if we are confident enough to act. What separates and defines heroes and cowards is the kind of action they take in spite of (or because of) their fear. The important thing is that they take the initiative to *act*. This means that it's possible to have courage and be afraid at the same time. This might explain why men on first dates say really dumb things that actually work in their favor.

I interviewed a Vietnam veteran who told me about a firefight he was in during his tour of duty. The shooting was constant, and he kept pulling the trigger on his M–16 like he was trained to do. In the course of returning fire, he turned to his side and saw that his friend had been shot in the head and killed. Try to imagine that fear.

With great shame, he realized that he couldn't stay there and keep shooting, so he made the decision to act and just ran. He escaped the horror of the bullets but not the guilt and shame that dominated his thoughts the next day. He feared that, by choosing flight over fight, he had failed in his duty. The irony is that he received a Purple Heart and a Silver Star medal. It seems that in his action, he headed the wrong way and ran directly into the oncoming fire. The troops around him perceived his encounter as one of the bravest things they'd ever seen. What he saw as cowardly, they saw as brave—not smart, but brave—all because of his willingness to take action. I guess any action can produce better results than no action. (Don't write that down.)

Another man I spoke with was called a hero in his small community because he had rushed into a burning building to save a child. But he told me that he didn't feel like a hero at all. The media had jumped on this story and was feeding the hero frenzy. The real story was that on the evening of the fire, he'd been feeling very low. He had lost custody of his child in an ugly divorce, he had lost his job, and he was struggling with alcohol. His life seemed filled with problems. He was temporarily staying with a friend, and when he heard the noise up the street, he walked over to see what was going on. People were screaming, pointing at the building, and saying they could hear the crying of a child trapped inside. The firefighters had been in the house but proclaimed it was unsafe for anyone to go in. Almost without hesitation, our hero soaked a blanket with a nearby hose, charged into the house, found the child, and carried him out of the building. But in telling me about this, he denied any bravery on his part. He admitted feeling nothing but fear the entire time! But he was more afraid for the child and the child's family, and that compelled him to act.

Both these stories show how people who are perceived as heroic and celebrated for bravery act while they are afraid. They didn't know exactly what had to be done, but they didn't hesitate to act. Fear can be paralyzing, but think about how many times in your life you have done well when you're afraid. I'm sure you can remember an example. So what is really stopping you from acting on this in business? You might want to occasionally take action while you're afraid and see how it feels. Who knows? It might feel a lot like confidence!

Ego and Self-Esteem

Many people have the mindset that if they just fix their problems, they will succeed. Top performers have a better approach. They know what strengths offer an advantage, eliminate the disadvantages that they cannot turn into an advantage, and avoid the perception of weaknesses. This sets the stage for their unfair fights, and they have the ego to enter the battle and win.

Wait, didn't I say that ego is often a disadvantage that needs to be reduced to turn it into an advantage? Yes, but you need that ego in order to be willing to act in the first place. Ego, like insecurity and self-preservation, can be a tool to facilitate action in certain circumstances. Many people we met succeeded in going from knowledge to implementation by attaching their goals directly to their egos and letting fear motivate them to discover and use their advantages.

Some top performers cannot tolerate not being rich, which in turn motivates them to do what most people would not or could not do to make sure that they always "make it." Technical engineers with few social skills might know that their technical projects are brilliant, but they must skirt their way around their fear to act and find a way to clearly present their projects to others. Conversely, appealing to someone's ego can also be a motivator. For example, customer service skills improve in a company where individual complaints toward employees are used as measures of job performance. It's amazing how fast someone will improve when you say during a performance review, "Two customers this week said that their experience with you in the store made them want to go home, find things they bought from us over the past year, and return them. So, regarding your performance, I think we have nowhere to go but up."

We asked a top oil company engineer how he achieved his innovations. He gave a complex answer about his decision-making process that set off my BS detector. When I pressed him, he admitted that his advantage was that he had mastered the ability to win the battle with himself. He wins *what* battle with himself? What does that mean? I wanted to tell him that there are a host of good medications that help with those kinds of things.

He explained that the battle he wins is over his own ego. Unlike a lot of people in his profession, this guy works under the assumption that every idea he has is incomplete and that he does not have all the answers. By embracing the idea that everyone knows something he doesn't, he isn't afraid to ask the stupid questions that everyone secretly wants the answers to but no one wants to ask for fear of seeming like they don't know what they're doing.

This guy knows he's smart and competent, and putting aside his confidence isn't easy for him. He doesn't want to be open about his lack of answers with colleagues whom he often considers bone-headed idiots. (It's hard to share your thoughts with people who don't have any.) But by winning the battle over his ego and putting aside the confidence he has in his own knowledge, he gets incredibly valuable information, input, and buy-in that give him an advantage and superior results. And then he implements them. Like all the top performers we met, he understands that it's not knowledge that yields power or guarantees results. The power comes from his ability to be open, to gather knowledge from others to enhance his projects beyond what he could do himself, and then to implement those projects.

Examining Your Belief System

People in the top 1 percent are driven by the knowledge that it's possible to project the personality and strength they need to succeed. They also know how to work around what stops them. This does not mean that they are full-of-it fakers who would trample old ladies to get ahead (regardless of how many cats they possess). Most top performers don't break the rules. They just know exactly where the line between good and the best is drawn, and they use every advantage they have to find a way to cross it.

One respondent used an unsolicited flirtation to his advantage: "I knew a lady who worked in a client's office, and she flirted with me every time I was there. I certainly didn't have an agenda, but by engaging a bit, I did get an unanticipated benefit: She gave me a bunch of information that I am sure other guys weren't getting. That information helped me land a giant account. I mean, I just had more information than anybody else." Acting on the flirtation to cheat on your wife or blackmail the employee? Unscrupulous. Engaging in it the way you would rub a friendly cat purring at your feet, while never indicating you actually want to take it home? Advantage. (That might be my worst analogy so far, but at least I was willing to implement it.)

Would some of this guy's competitors be inclined to look at his behavior with disdain or resentment? Of course—but he cannot worry about these things. It does not matter whether they are jealous or just feel it was grossly manipulative. They're simply justifying why they themselves didn't succeed at landing the account. They lost that fight and need to rationalize their failure; they need to view the successful person as "bad" in order to justify their own unwillingness to either respond to the woman's flirtatiousness or find some other advantage to implement. They then can use that reasoning to justify their lack of advancement and stay at the same station and financial situation forever. I'm sure your loser buddy we learned about in Chapter 5 has deployed a few of these excuses.

It's like the father who tells his son, "I don't know why you need to go to that there college. After all, working in the underground sawmill-slaughterhouse-coal mine was good enough for my father, for me, and for your brothers, so why shouldn't it be good enough for you?" Okay, I'm being melodramatic—there are no underground sawmill-slaughterhouse-coal mines. But if there were, the people who work there would be proud, bloody, coughing, and squinting. Generations of them with no ability to see the advantages you see.

When I was growing up, my father called this "blue-collar BS." To justify your feelings about your own existence and your unwillingness to move out of a mediocre situation because of the effort and risks that might be involved, you simply find something wrong with people who have or want something better—and dismiss them when they act on their advantage. Better to be poor, honest, and loyal than to be rich, deceptive, and stepping on people (as if these are the only options). This kind of thinking excuses anyone from pursuing positions of greater responsibility so as not to be seen as a traitor by their friends and coworkers. It is the foundation of every "us-against-them" mentality.

This is how a person's belief system holds him or her back. If you see managers as inherently bad people, you will never become "the enemy." Instead you'll stay in positions of lower pay and lower authority. This kind of logic is almost its own form of insanity. Think back to Chapter 4; this is not the power of thinking negatively—this is a defeatist attitude! If you start viewing people who are successful as having achieved success only by doing bad things or being bad people, you have a misguided moral code that will prevent you from ever being a top performer. You have to get past all these traditional notions of class and fairness and define what you need to succeed, not be limited by how other people define you. If you believe that the people in control are inherently evil, it will literally take a revolution for *you* to be in control. Unfortunately, rebellions require that you suffer for your advantage for a while—*and* you have to make your own flag!

So What's in Your Way?

Top performers understand that it is not only embracing what your advantage is but using that advantage that makes the difference. In other words, knowing what to do and actually doing it are not at all the same thing. A lot of people know a lot and do very little. What's stopping you from doing something with what *you* know? Do you have the willingness to examine your life and your motives? To identify your advantages and actually use them? To step outside your comfort zone and act in spite of the fear?

Sit down with a piece of paper and write down three things that block you from taking action. Are they tangible things? Real obstacles you'd have to do something to get around? What caused them? It's possible that you're held back by some feeling or experience from long ago—a problem, an issue, a tragedy—buried so deep that you don't really think about it every day.

Second-Level Lesson

Making the leap from knowing to doing is less about being willing and more about being action-oriented.

A lot of seemingly unwilling people are put in positions where they would have to take action—and they do. But there are also a lot of very willing people who would never take action. The belief that taking action is what you're supposed to be doing is what causes people to really get things done. The people who are most successful are not the people who hesitated and didn't get on the boat. They got on the boat. Now maybe they made a mistake and sank the boat, but they were on that boat. Doing something is much more effective than strategically thinking of tasks that do not lead to action. There's really no way to *try* to jump off a bridge. You're either in the process of jumping or not. Being indecisive is based on the fear of not making the right decision. The most successful people that we saw might have felt indecisive, complained, and waffled, but they took action. They might make mistakes, but they make mistakes while taking action. The world is full of very competent, well-thought-out ideas that no one ever pulled the trigger on. Not only is knowledge not power; when it comes to getting things done, it's often irrelevant.

If you're afraid or unwilling, you need to explore whether that fear or reluctance is seated in something you can choose to overcome. When fear or reluctance seems immovable, maybe taking a look at the worst-case scenario is what finally moves you forward. The worst-case scenario is not failure at the attempted test; it's looking back and realizing you weren't willing to act in the window of opportunity. If you find that you truly are unwilling, are you satisfied with living the rest of your life as a person who's unwilling? If you are completely satisfied with your unwillingness to act, you could be a rare spiritual giant or a new form of superloser who has the power to demotivate the masses. And if you are that powerful, maybe you should just suck it up and take action.

A lot of successful people have something in common: It's failure! In contrast, what a lot of *unsuccessful* people have in common is the admission that "I didn't do anything when I had the opportunity to really do *something*." We've got a name for that; it's called whining!

What "something" are you willing to do? Here are some important steps to moving past obstacles that prevent you from implementing your advantage.

Define Your Goals

If you are willing to do more than examine your life and your motives and commit to implementing a plan of action, you need to define your goals. This is crucial to crossing the line from recognizing your advantage to actually implementing it. Think of goals as gas for your car: The car is designed to take you where you want to go, but without gas you are not going anywhere.

You need to identify what it is that you are going to do and then outline how you will do it: Define your goals and then *write them down*. Writing is power. Only 3 percent of the population—among them almost all of our top performers—have written out their goals. No wonder that 3 percent have the majority of the money and make the majority of the decisions in our world. By writing your goals down, you will know where you are going and create a map to refer to in the event you get lost. Who wants to stop and ask for directions on the road to success? Especially when 97 percent of your roadside advisors don't have a map!

Remember that advice I got on goal setting from the cranky old guy years ago: "You know, if you want to be a good guitar player, you ain't gonna get there carving wooden ducks." If I want to be really good at what I do, I actually have to practice what I do. Words on paper separate fact from fiction and help me focus consistently on what I need to practice. Some people say, "My goals are in my head." The truth is that your head is full of goo just like everyone else's and you need to write things down.

Manage Stress

Stress comes with success. And most of the top performers we interviewed understood the real cause of their stress and broke it down like this: The leading definition of stress is knowing exactly what you should be doing, yet constantly doing something else.

Let's say that my lovely wife asks me to go down to Whole Foods to get her a $5 apple because obviously only a Whole Foods $5 apple will do. So there I go, off to Whole Foods on a really nice Saturday afternoon like the good husband I am. On my way, I pass by this place that is like a bar, and I pop in for a moment. Okay, it's not *like* a bar, it *is* a bar—and it's got every sport available on big-screen TVs, and before I know it, I'm sitting there with a drink in hand, sports on TV, and I'm talking to the very lovely, 25-year-old waitress Heather. It should be nirvana, but I realize that I am beginning to feel very stressed. How is that possible?

It's possible because I'm not doing what I am supposed to be doing, and I know it. But, still, I don't stop doing it. Instead, my mind starts to compromise: Maybe I could get Heather the waitress to run to Whole Foods for me. Maybe I could go to Whole Foods and take Heather the waitress with me. (Okay, bad idea.)

The problem is that I know what I should be doing, but I'm not doing it, and I get stressed. Someone once told me that he wanted to get married in the next five years but didn't have the first idea what to do to achieve that goal. Step one: Start dating! "If you want to get married in the next five years," I told him, "stop going to Star Trek conventions. There are no women there! You have to take actions that have a chance of getting you where you want to go."

$$Knowledge - effective\ action = stress$$

This is not the formula for success.

Don't Fear Success

Fear of success is a catch phrase you hear thrown around a lot. I'm not sure I believe it. Actually, I think it's a complete misnomer. *Fear of success* literally means that someone is afraid of everything going well and living happily ever after. I don't really think that is what people fear. I think fear goes more like this:

- I'll reach my goal, and then I will fail or fall apart.
- I'll become wealthy, and then I'll become evil.
- I will get the girl or guy I want, and then they'll die.

Hmmm, maybe I've been watching too many soap operas. But still the concept of "fear of success" really sounds much more like fear of the failure that you believe inevitably follows any success. You have the fear in the back of your mind that if success comes to you, either you're going to screw it up or it's going to screw you up. That type of thinking is not so much fear of success as it is a raging fear of failure. I met a young actress who said that she was afraid to become a movie star because she might end up in a reality TV show being filmed while she was in rehab. (She was pretty tipsy when she said that.)

Fear, as we know, can be powerful. It can make you act or paralyze you. And no amount of knowledge is going to make you get over it. Some people will say, "Well, I really need more information to make my decision." That's how you get shot in the head in a firefight. Our research shows that not only was knowledge not the key to success, but in many cases having too much knowledge was what kept people from achieving success. Think back on one of your more difficult accomplishments. I'm sure it was hard to achieve, and maybe you had no idea at the onset how difficult the challenges would be, but remember that you're thinking about it now because you did it. If you had never tried it, you could not now enjoy the success that resulted from it.

If you want to be successful, you have to get real with yourself about fear, accept the risks and rewards of every action, and consider what failure really means. It does not mean the end of your life. In fact, it's the beginning of success. Use your advantages to fight the fear and move past it. Otherwise, you'll have to deal with the seemingly idiotic condition of being afraid of fear.

Manage the People around You

As we saw in Chapter 5, our top 1 percent understood that you have to spend time with people who can position you to succeed. Accepting that is quite simply a matter of telling yourself, "I'm going to get real about the people I'm hanging out with." If you hang out with a bunch of unmotivated losers, you'll be hard-pressed to make the top 1 percent. If you need an example, look at how well it worked out for NFL star Michael Vick, a talented guy who let his career literally go to the dogs.

In the workplace, success eludes many people despite their best efforts, but usually it comes down to the willingness to manage three things: what your boss thinks is important, what you say, and especially the people who work with and for you.

How do you get recognized as a good employee? Hard work? Dedication? Well, yes, to some extent. But just as writing down your goals is essential, the best employees will write down the top five things their boss thinks is important that month and make sure everything they do is connected to one of those five things. You could do something remarkable that changes the world for the better, but unless your boss thinks changing the world is a priority, you'll still get a poor review. You might even get fired with the Nobel Peace Prize hanging around your neck while the no-talent fool across the hall gets promoted for being focused on goals he does not fully understand.

Be mindful about getting in your boss's mind (even if it means learning to think like an idiot). People who are really successful have the advantage of understanding that it's not just about being good at what you do; you also have to understand what your superiors believe "good" actually is. And then you have to do it—even if it is not what you value most. A lot of people don't understand how coworkers who aren't very good at their jobs get better reviews than they do. But think back to the guy who complimented everyone in the company and consequently was promoted: If what you do is in line with what your boss thinks is important, you're going to succeed in the boss's eyes. To some people, this is called "sucking up," but it's a lot better than sucking so bad at making your boss see your value that you are first on the chopping block when it's time for layoffs. The point is not to worry about the opinions of those you pass by on your way to the executive restroom.

And on your way there, manage everything that comes out of your mouth. Your words define you just as much as your actions do (sometimes even more!). Some people could be top performers, but what they say and how they say it holds them back; conversely, there are those who don't perform at all but what they say is fantastic and overshadows their lackluster performance. People want to believe that it's not what you say; it's what you do. Well, often the people around you don't have the ability to see the big picture and know all that you do; so it very well might be what you *say* that holds the impact. How you present yourself and how you explain things can influence how people define you. But that needs to be true all the time, not just in the big moments. If you always say something stupid, then people always see you through a filter of stupidity.

Yet just sucking up to the boss and shutting up won't be enough. Being able to understand and manage coworkers is a large component of success. It is more essential than ever to manage how people feel about their working environment. If people don't like their surroundings, they are much more likely not to like you. Being a maverick who does things "old school" looks really cool in the movies, but don't kid yourself. Let's break that term down: "old" as in *possibly obsolete* and "school" as in *still in training*. Not a good combo! This does not exactly set you up as influential.

Today's business world looks much different from your grandfather's. You have men and women of every race, ethnicity, age, and class background. Successful people deal with this head-on. They don't cling to any line of thinking that says that whatever *they* are (whatever sex, race, generation, etc., they might be) is better. They don't shy away from diversity or fear the challenges of being responsible for it. They simply have the willingness to manage it.

Are you willing to embrace change and understand that the world is different? For example, if you are in your forties or older, you might find it impossible to comprehend that a 25-year-old would quit her job to go on a ski trip. Or how about the 21-year-old we interviewed who said, "The reason I'm trying to get this job is to pay for my Jeep Cherokee, and if I work too late I don't have time to drive it, so I'm not taking the job"? If you're over 40, you might wonder how someone could be that irresponsible. "Kids these days just don't have the same work ethic! Back in my day, we ate dirt and liked it. We walked to school. Uphill. Both ways. In snow. In Florida. As a matter of fact, back in my day, we had no shoes. Hell—we had no feet! We just walked on our nubs. All we had were nubs back then. Didn't get feet until 1971."

By aggrandizing (gotta love that word) our own ideals and work habits and trivializing other people's, we fail to understand what those people can contribute to the workplace and we fail to manage their expectations. Believe me, that aggrandizement/trivialization occurs on both sides of the generation gap. Do you know how people in their twenties and thirties view those in their forties and above? They say, "Mr. Wynn, the reason your computer crashes is because you're old." I actually had some young guy say to me, "Sir, when I asked you that question, I wanted the answer, not the history of the answer."

What causes this disparity in outlook and values? There are two significant factors: how we were raised and how we were taught.

When older generations started school, their teachers said, "Welcome to first grade. Here is the curriculum. You complete it, and if you do well, you'll get a gold star." When younger generations went to school, their teachers said, "Welcome to first grade. We love you, we care about you, and we're not going to leave you behind. We've got multiple things that we're working on. We're going to work on this for a little while, then we'll work on that for a little while, then we're going to stop and take a break. We are going to celebrate our accomplishments on the way to the goal, and everybody gets a trophy regardless of accomplishment." They created this approach to help build self-esteem in the children—and it did—but it also resulted in some of these young people having more self-esteem and sense of entitlement than actual talents or abilities.

Then there are the lies about success our parents tell us. Remember back in Chapter 1, I showed how parents tell kids that they can be anybody they want to be and do anything they want to do. Now those kids have come to collect on what they were told and what they've been given all along the way. Parents of Generation X and Generation Y weren't around as much as parents of previous generations were around for their kids, and so they gave their children more to compensate for their lack of engagement. They felt guilty. Guilty parents raise narcissistic children. It doesn't mean they are bad kids; it just means that we can expect certain behaviors from kids raised that way.

The best approach to managing diverse generations—the only approach, really—is to manage them in the same way they grew up. You can't take a 25-year-old and—snap!—make him 40. The older generations come in early, work long hours, and take their work home. The younger generations value their personal time much more than work achievements, which is why someone would quit a job to take a one-time rafting trip. We might be quick to think they can change ("After all, I was young once!"), but it really isn't the same today. When I was young, sex wouldn't kill you, and I could litter and still feel good about myself. No one constantly told me that I was personally responsible for the planet. So how can I say I know exactly what a 20-year-old is going through today? I'm still trying to figure out why it's so important for them to have their underwear showing.

The willingness to be open-minded and to understand how the generations perceive and value the workplace is an advantage you can use to be successful in any environment. The bottom line is that these young people aren't living in our times; we are living in theirs. Younger workers have more options today. The older generations need to adjust accordingly. If you can't find the willingness to embrace and manage the future, then you don't *have* a future. There are 70 million young people coming into the workforce, and 50 percent of the entire existing workforce will retire in the next 15 years or so. What does that tell you? It means that we of the older generation probably won't get to set the standards for office conduct. Not gonna happen!

In my company, we started accommodating younger generations by dropping the dress code. Do you know what happens when you drop the dress code in Houston, Texas? I've got naked people working for me. But it works because young people don't like to "dress" for work and being comfortable inspires productivity. So when one of my competitors called to ask why all of his young people were leaving to join my company, I said, "Because we're all naked!" Of course, he hung up.

Think again about the loser buddies in Chapter 5 and the importance of getting off the horse that brought you. Just like you need to make the hard decisions to get away from people who hold you back and to connect with people who can help you, you need to be willing to change in order to manage, not just manage through change.

Willingness to Change

It's a simple thing: Sometimes we can't make things happen unless we can summon the willingness to say, "Wait a second. This is *my* life. Whatever I'm capable of, I should be allowed to take a shot without someone else's voice and opinions standing in my way." We talked to top performers who gave credit to the people in their past but didn't hesitate to move on. They weren't guilt-ridden. They simply realized that to get where they intended to go, they couldn't stay tethered to people who weren't going to take them there. The top 1 percent do not drag their business baggage with them into the future.

We often have feelings of guilt, remorse, and low self-esteem that tell us we owe our existence to other people. How can we owe someone our future? Loyalty is valuable if it works for both parties. But loyalty that robs you of your freedom is slavery. We should be loyal to people and situations that let us thrive and not to those that don't. The most successful people say, "Thank you! I will never forget you as I move forward with my life."

Most people lack the will to take action and change their ways until they've reached a precipice or gotten their butts kicked. Then, when it's time to change, most people just replace bad habits with good ones—they switch addictions, so to speak. I switched from smoking to eating fruit. My house looks and smells like a luau on the weekends, but that stale cigarette odor is gone!

Willingness is more than having the willpower to change. Sometimes, it means changing your perspective on the problem. Our interviews with the top 1 percent showed that they did not overcome bad habits simply through willpower; they overcame them with better, productive habits. They placed the power of their will where it did some good! If they found themselves worrying too much, they stopped; but when worry was a valid part of a solution, they used it. Worry in the right direction creates preparedness.

If you can't stop complaining, become a politician. If you can't stop lying, become a criminal defense attorney. If you find fault with every little thing you see, become a safety inspector. One top performer replaced sticking his nose in all of his employees' business with sticking his nose in his competitor's business. He went from being just plain annoying to being productively annoying—and very successful.

Think back to some of the top performers we mention in the book; you'll remember that these supersuccessful people first acknowledged how an advantage could help them and then exercised the will to act on that knowledge. They willed themselves to implement their edge.

- The insurance salesman from Chapter 2 was willing to acknowledge that people perceived him as not sharp enough to rip anybody off, and he was willing to use that perception to build gigantic trust.
- Mr. Likable from Chapter 4 knew that positive talk gained him popularity in high school; he was willing to apply that strategy in business to help advance him from the mailroom to CEO.
- The Realtor from Chapter 5 was willing to ask her husband for that valuable list and exploit the edge it gave her.

If you've worked hard to identify or create an advantage that can earn you some measure of success, why squander it by coming up short on the will to *use* it? Your willingness to implement your personal advantage, whatever it may be, gives you the power to change your station or status.

Getting people to a state of willingness is like driving senior citizens around town. They might read the billboard signs out loud as you drive by, treat you like you're 11 years old, tell you there used to be a better route to take back when they drove a Packard, and give you detailed accounts of their most prominent ailments. But they have earned the right to this behavior by surviving what the world has thrown their way. Regardless of your age (you might be too young to know what a Packard is), if you are this far along in the book, you have earned the right to interpret, judge, compare, and complain about your experience so far. I accept this, based on the time you've put in. So all that is left for you to do is to cross the line and take action before you die of old age.

9

———

Action and Adaptability
Create Opportunity

———

Establish a repeatable process for success

MARRIAGE IS FATTENING. MARRIED COUPLES LIKE TO SNACK. You're home, you spend time together, it's always like Thanksgiving. But if you're single and trying to attract a mate, you're trying to get down to a "dating weight." The stuff in your refrigerator starts to smell as leftovers go uneaten, and you find yourself going to the gym just to be around people. So if you're married and want to lose weight, maybe spending less time together, dating outside your marriage, or getting a divorce would be the most practical ways of doing it. Maybe these are not the preferred ways of slimming down, but they should work.

Getting a divorce to lose weight, although probably effective, is not a strategy most of us would choose. But we embrace every other equally ridiculous truth about dieting from experts who claim you can lose weight and still eat all your favorite foods if you buy this pill or that machine. Somehow we believe that pills or machines combined with miracle meal plans will magically make us into ideal physical specimens with little actual effort: "We'll just ship you food.

We can ship food right to you!" Apparently, the key to weight loss is having someone FedEx you French fries.

While we might like to believe these diet experts' pitches, they're just not true. It's like being on an airplane when a flight attendant tells you that in the event of a water landing, your seat will become a flotation device. Well, planes don't land in water; they land in airports. They *crash* in water. A pilot never says, "The airport is so crowded that in order to make sure you can all make your connecting flights, we're going to land in the bay." That's just not true. But the attendant never tells you where to find your flotation device in the event of a water *crash* because, although the phrasing would be accurate, the truth it reflects is tremendously unpopular.

The truth about success is often unpopular too. We say we want to know the truth about becoming successful. But when we hear the truth about success, it can be a tough pill to swallow, even for those who make it to the top. So we come up with different "truths" about success—that is, lies. We're back where we started in Chapter 1: We'd rather believe the myths about success over the harsh realities. We want to think people are successful—and *they* want us to think they're successful—based on what we've always heard creates success. Remember the lies and funky smells of those initial interview answers we revealed in Chapter 2. We think, "If I'm smart enough, work hard enough, think strategically enough, listen well enough. . . . If I'm all those things, then regardless of anything else and no matter who I am, I will be successful."

The real truth is that it takes a lot more work than merely working hard, no matter how unpopular that reality may be. It's difficult to face and embrace your own shortcomings. And it's not always pretty. We like to tell people the cool stories that make us look fantastic. I often want to tell people I'm successful because I'm just so darned good at a number of important things, but the truth is that I'm not that darned good! Most people aren't. We just have to be willing to do what it takes and do it again, even if it means we have to own up to what we're no good at. So am I, personally, smart? I think I am. People say that I am. But I'm not the most focused person; I've got some ADD issues. There are a lot of things I'm really terrible at! I once worked at a company that instituted a regulation requiring someone to go in the file room with me if I were going to put files away. They knew that if they left me in there alone, they would never find those files again.

The top 1 percent we interviewed looked at the business world as it really is: unfair. Then they confronted the ugly truths about themselves, were honest about them, and used what they found to their advantage. They limited their disadvantages, discovered or created personal advantages, and were willing to use them. Then they found a way to repeat the process and win again and again. I'm not saying that the top performers are all about winning. In general, they would not have a problem losing if it were to their advantage to lose. I talked to a corporate leader who said losing at golf with the right people had definitely helped his career. He did not *try* to play badly, and he had very good form. He just did not win enough to make his type A personality more than his colleagues could bear.

One top performer we interviewed explained how he went from midlevel mediocrity to the most productive midlevel manager in his company within one year through willingness to face his own limitations and then take them to the next level. Until then, this manager had wracked his brain to come up with methods that would hold his frontline supervisors more accountable for results, but his ideas weren't very effective. He wasn't much of an idea man, or at least the right kind of idea man. His ideas blended corny, stupid, and uncomfortable in a remarkable way. He once had his blue-collar supervisors take a cake-baking class to get them to understand the recipe for success. Yes, really. So his team knew he cared, albeit in a disturbing way.

Then, one of his people said, "You're really good at making people feel important. Why don't you do what comes naturally?" The manager realized that he knew a good idea when he heard it; he just didn't have any of his own. So he embraced this as an advantage. He ditched Duncan Hines, and in its place he implemented celebration meetings with the supervisors to point out what they did well. He had them discuss what, as a group, they thought they could improve. Then he sat back and let them create a plan together. Results went through the roof.

In the end, this top performer stopped trying to be what he was not (a creative idea man) and started using what he was (a guy who excelled at making people feel important) to help his team to come up with its own solutions. His boss thought he was a genius and asked, "Do you have any more great ideas?" He did. He was prepared to repeat the process at a higher level: "Yes. We'll have a middle managers' idea meeting every month, and I will facilitate." So maybe knowledge really is power; it just doesn't have to be your knowledge.

Do your natural traits help you move forward? Maybe your advantage can help you create momentum and forge an opportunity where you might not have thought one existed. If you're easily bored, maybe that's the catalyst. Obviously the guy who invented the Slinky must have been absolutely bored out of his mind and happened to have a lot of scrap metal. And as I said before, I'm fairly sure the person who invented air-conditioning was just some really sweaty guy disturbed by and seeking relief from his prolific perspiration.

You need to know how and when to use your advantage to get the opportunity you're looking for. As I said in Chapter 8, if you've gotten this far, you should be ready and willing to act on your advantages. Be patient for the right opportunity. Impatient people have a lot of problems, among them inaction. They get so busy being busy that they sometimes get nothing accomplished. Look carefully for the unfair fight that works for you. Successful people know how to act quickly to seize an opportunity, but they also know when to use their personal advantage and act to create the greatest opportunity. Then they consistently couple that advantage with their skills and constantly make adjustments as circumstances warrant. Doing all this can move you past 99 percent of your industry peers and into the top 1 percent.

You've unlocked your secret advantage; you're willing to use it. The key now is to understand how to act and keep acting and adapting to create opportunities.

First-Level Lesson

The real truth about success is that not only do we not like to talk about the real truth, but we don't necessarily want to hear it.

In *The Matrix*, Keanu Reeves's character discovers that, basically, the world he thinks he's living in is false. He actually lives, or is kept alive, anyway, in another world that's much worse and more difficult to deal with, let alone overcome—and it took a whole trilogy ripe with cheesy special effects for that to happen. But getting there required higher-level tactics, ones he had to learn to think his way through. What was in front of him and what was real were completely different. It's like a restaurant with the pictures of the food displayed on the wall. When your entrée comes out, it does not remotely resemble the photo or even, in many cases, food. Even if the real truth about success is less palatable than you've pictured, you have to digest it if you want to benefit from it.

Cut Out Random Factors and Fluctuations

Before you can act and raise the bar on success, it's helpful to assess just where that bar lies. Pulitzer Prize–winning author Leonard Mlodinow argues in his book *The Drunkard's Walk: How*

Randomness Rules Our Lives that people have a baseline for performance. All of us at times will dip above or below that line regardless of any coaching, praise, or criticism we get. Sometimes you do a really, really great job. The next time out you might not do so well because you've just recently performed so far above your norm. So if you exceed expectations in one case and then wonder why you didn't do as well the next time, it's because you're coming back to your norm. And if you perform horribly, just flat-out terrible, you might notice you do a lot better the next go-round because you're going back toward your norm.

This explains the confusion that results when someone does a praiseworthy job ("Hey, you're doing fantastic! Congratulations!") and then falls flat the next time around. The accolades aren't to blame; the person's just shifting back to a performance baseline. Conversely, when someone does a horrible job ("Man, you better get your @%#! act together. That's terrible!") and then gets a lot better, the boss thinks, "Hey, yelling obscenities at people makes them perform better, and I've finally found a leadership style that comes naturally to me." The truth is that this person performed so far below the norm that there was nowhere to go but up.

Your personal advantage can change that. Mlodinow's theory suggests that no matter what kind of leadership communication style you use (be it positive affirmation or calling your employees idiots), things happen in a way that is more or less up and down, and you'll always get more or less the same results. You might occasionally rise above the norm, but you're never going to sustain being better until you change something. In other words, you really need a *repeatable* advantage that can raise your norm to a higher place. When you can apply your personal advantage in a repeatable way, you raise the bar and keep it from falling back. That new height of success becomes your new baseline. In other words, you are taking the randomness out of randomness at random in order to improve normal. (Yeah, that sentence just happened.)

The Gallup Institute study I first cited in Chapter 4 actually concurs with this. While it calls talent the main ingredient to success, it also describes talent as a natural, recurring pattern that can be productively applied. That's what a personal advantage is! Gallup's and our research both suggest that intelligence and skills are not enough to guarantee success. Knowing how to ride a skateboard is skill; having the balance to be superior at it is talent. That's essentially how dumb people with talent rule the world and why smart people work for them. It's also why the top skateboarders in the world start most of their sentences with the word "Dude!"

For example, writing, research, expertise, rehearsing, and testing material on other groups can prepare you to deliver a great speech. You can have the confidence to get up there and believe you will do well. But when you do, if you can't read the members of your audience, you'll have problems feeling what they feel as you speak. You'll fail to make that connection with the front row and trigger the usual chain reaction of acceptance and focus. You can't make people listen to you if they don't like the direction you are heading. As you hit the 15-minute mark, that audience will slowly start to lose the will to live. You're not a great speaker; you just have a good speech. You are, in fact, informed, on point, and hopelessly boring.

The top 1 percent tend to feel their way through things in a way that others cannot and in a way that cannot be taught. They understand that what you believe and how you handle fear of the unknown allows you to capitalize on your advantage. Then you can avoid random fluctuations and you can control and endure the down times when no one wins. My parents and grandparents made it through the Great Depression and ended up, well, cheap! My Aunt Ethel was so old when she died (of course, you already know she was old because there are no young people named Ethel) that she'd endured enough for two lifetimes of fluctuation, including the Depression. She used to say that money was worth more than you could buy with it. She had to say that. What else could she say?

("I'm psychotically frugal?") When she passed away, we spent her money—the money she'd amassed because she thought it was too valuable to spend. (Let me tell you, we enjoyed it. No money spends better than the cash you didn't earn.)

If you just had the worst day of your life, chances are pretty slim that tomorrow will be worse. If you hate this whole chapter of my book, you are bound to like the next one better. That's not a guarantee; it's just more likely. (Fact is, Chapter 10 is really short and it's the last chapter, so maybe I'm hedging the bet a little bit, but still you get my point.) If today you play the greatest golf game of your life, next time you might want to bring your waders, a few extra balls, and maybe an extra putter for when you smash one in frustration.

But if you use your personal advantage to adapt and guide you through those inevitable fluctuations, you are simply more likely to succeed. Lowering your expectations of people and circumstances usually leads to happiness. I think Buddha said that, or maybe it was Tom Cruise. But as you recall, happiness isn't the point. A key advantage to exceeding expectations is by controlling them to begin with.

Adjust in Midflight

Business, like life, is similar to landing an airplane on an aircraft carrier. It's a moving target. Success has plenty to do with knowing where that target is and using the skills you have developed to get there. But skills will get you only so far. The rest is determined by how you come in and feel it out as you go. You need to be acutely aware of your surroundings and flexible when necessary. You almost never hear someone say, "The key to success is rigidity." That's how your plane ends up in the water. Life and business, like those jets, move and shift, and things snap if they're too rigid—whether it's a bridge, your emotions, or your sanity.

Don't get me wrong: You cannot fly that plane without qualifications, and you must follow a basic process to land. There is value in processes—the way they help us stack things in neat little piles and set up systems for the flow of information and production. A process is a guarantee: Everybody can follow its rules and know on a certain level what he or she must do. There's a lot more to success than just process. In the long term, when facing constantly moving targets, we must adapt.

To adapt, we must be more than willing to change. We must actually do it. My father is 79 years old, and he's really fantastic with a computer—totally computer literate and nearly 80. Four years ago he was not. Four years ago, my dad sent me his first e-mail. It read: "Dammit!" That's all it said. Now he buys all of our family's Christmas presents online. Of course, he bought me a nightgown and my wife a chainsaw—he *is*, after all, 79 years old.

My father knows that action and adaptability create opportunity. I asked him, "Why in the world would you want to learn to use a computer after being a retired corporate chief all these years?" He answered, "I didn't like living in a world where the tool of the day was beyond me. I didn't want to live in a world where everybody uses this tool every single day that I was afraid to touch. So I called a guy on the phone, and he went out and bought a computer for me. Then I hired him to teach me how to use it. And within four or five days, I could send e-mail and communicate on a computer." (Of course, there was a bit of a learning curve. I think the second e-mail I got from him was a simple "Help!" But he embraced the tool, even with some initial frustration.)

So are you willing to pick up and use the tool of the day—to adjust your mindset and get real about success? Then make sure you are in a place where your personal advantage gives you an edge.

I once worked at Pizza Inn as a teenager. Yes, I worked at Pizza Inn because apparently I didn't have the right stuff to work at Pizza

Hut. I was fired for incompetence. My manager, not quite the embodiment of competence himself, told me, "You just don't care!" But my idea of caring simply did not conform to his idea of caring. I liked to make funny pizza dough animals and show them to kids at the window. That's not the goal of the pizza business, it seems. I didn't have a lot of what it took to keep customers happy and buying great pizza, so I used what I had. I had the creativity to make funny pizza animals with eyes made of pepperoni. There was also the ill-fated Swiss cheese pizza incident, which forced everyone to evacuate the building (innovative and smelly). That creativity helps me today in my business, so that was and remains a usable skill. If that guy hadn't fired me, if he hadn't called me out on skills or talents I lacked for that position, I might still be working at Pizza Inn. I could still be there, struggling along as a person with some other commendable skills that just happened to be wrong for the job.

It's the basic success formula: Right person + wrong role = little chance of superstardom. Or even mere stardom. Really all that equation gets you is just a lot of reprimands from your supervisor. ("Wynn! You could have topped five pizzas with the pepperoni you've used to give sight to these doughy possum things piling up over here." "Dude, they're porcupines. See the toothpick quills?" The guy had no vision.)

In the course of taking action, you must adapt to your circumstances and develop your abilities to create opportunities. Are you flexible enough to tweak your advantage to the opportunity at hand? If you're not strong in strategic thinking but have a quick mind and thrive in situations that call for thinking on your feet, an environment where quick response is valued over great overall vision would be a better fit. If your sights aren't set on being a CEO or managing a bunch of VPs responsible for rolling out some enormous, ground-shaking, long-term project, manage a team of air traffic controllers. In that scenario, you have to be quick on your feet, and reaction time is crucial.

In our interviews with top performers, we essentially discovered two means to achieving the same successful end: People were either natural seat-of-the-pants impatient leaders or gifted strategic thinkers accustomed to a calm, patient approach. In the end, you get the same result—finding solutions to the task at hand.

It's hard to live your life based on other people's vision and values. You've got to base it on your own. Successful people don't follow some semimythical track for success that they're not qualified to follow. The top performers we interviewed know that the real truth about success is being able to act in ways you know you can. If you attempt something you simply can't do or aren't in the role that values what you're doing well, it doesn't matter how good you are at it. Working really hard in a direction in which you consistently prove to be mediocre just makes you a dedicated annoyance. But being the best at something that no one needs makes you an irrelevant expert!

If I'm thick-skinned, maybe I situate myself around people with sensitive egos. In that setting, thick skin is valuable or an advantageous asset. Hollywood might be a good place for me; people in the entertainment industry are notoriously sensitive and tend to overreact. But some thick-skinned people fare pretty well. Clint Eastwood had a lot of problems, including being branded as just not being talented enough. They told Clint Eastwood he wasn't a good actor. And if you watch some of his early TV roles and movies, they might not exactly "make your day."

He's a go-getting, tough guy, and not just in the movies. He's naturally thick-skinned. In the face of difficult situations and doubters, he won't fold. He keeps moving forward. Despite being labeled mediocre, he never crumbled, and the fact that his career grew is a reflection of his determination. Early in his career, no one ever would have guessed that he would win an Academy Award (*maybe* a People's Choice Award), much less make a slew of Academy Award–nominated movies. He avoided a lot of problems that actors and directors typically have by not having a prima donna mindset.

Not aspiring to Hollywood greatness? That doesn't mean you can't turn your advantage into greatness a little closer to home. Perhaps you should partner with somebody who doesn't have the same skills. A lot of times we work amid people who essentially know the same stuff we know, so knowledge won't set us apart. A unique take is a useful advantage that shows you have or might offer something valuable. How valuable is what you have to offer if the eight people around you offer the same thing? As simple as it sounds, a lot of people are very successful merely because they've found a way to thrive in an uncompetitive arena, and their personal advantages keep them there.

Despite my football foibles from earlier chapters, I've been a valued athlete twice in my life. The first time was when I went from playing school sports in the 4A division down to 1A. "Oooh!" I thought, "A star is born." When I moved down to 1A, suddenly I was the best guy in the league. The same thing happened when I played A League softball and started on a team that had won a championship. I was only an okay player, but I started on the best team in the best league. No one was going to single me out for my skills and talent. I just filled a role. A few years later, age and injuries forced me to drop to the D League. Suddenly, I was a star. They could have built a shrine for me in D League. Sure, most of the players were kind of drunk, but still—I excelled in D League. The point is that sometimes success is simply determined by the arena you're in. Why would you think you can compete in an area that's really competitive when you could find one that isn't? More importantly, why wouldn't you want to start by capitalizing on this less competitive arena? It may sound personally demeaning, but isn't the reason you're reading this book to fix the fight to your advantage?

You need to be honest about where you fit into the marketplace. Find an arena where the skill, strategy, process, or advantage you have is not the same thing everyone else has. Win a few unfair fights. Learn to act and adapt to the inevitable problems and fluctuations you will face there and create new opportunities. Then test your personal advantage and use it to create a repeatable process that will allow you to stay focused on success because you are good at what you do even on your worst days. On your good days you are, as one top performer from Mississippi put it, "as dominant as a rollin' ball of butcher knives."

Without a repeatable process in place, our assumptions shape our relationships. They limit our vision and reduce the impact of our knowledge and experience. If you're already looking for areas where you can use your advantages, you'll eventually see patterns emerge. Remember, though, that a repeatable process has to be something you can actually maintain. The more moving parts something has, the more likely it is to break down. If something is too complex, it can't be maintained. It's like my mother's cooking when I was growing up; it was very ambitious, just not consistently edible. Admittedly, she tended to leave out certain ingredients because they were so much trouble the last time. And even though she managed our expectations by saying, "Tonight's meal is largely experimental and I'll accept no negative comments," her culinary efforts did not match the consistency of her love. A repeatable process for success must be easy to sustain. At times, that requires the flexibility to create the exact opportunities you're after. Results are more important than sticking to the process, so be mindful that even the best process or system has to be flexible enough to adapt to the task before you. Action and flexibility create opportunity.

Connecting the Dots: Upon Reflection

Thinking back on all the conversations and interviews I have had with top performers, I find it interesting that most of the success stories feature relatively normal people who simply did some things a little differently, not abnormally. They did not take the road less traveled; they took the right road at the right time with the right people. They didn't just do what someone else told them to do; they discovered, evaluated, and seized opportunities that would really help them be successful. Of course, as you remember, they didn't tell us that right away either. In Chapter 2, we saw how almost all of the top performers, regardless of their industry, initially gave similar pat answers about the reasons for their success. We pressed harder to get the real answers. That pressing ("No offense, but people who suck told us exactly the same thing . . .") along with the promise of anonymity loosened their tongues to produce the *real* truth about success.

I've pressed you pretty hard in this book too. So it's time for your moment of truth: Are you ready to connect the dots? Are you ready to change?

Second-Level Lesson

What it takes to get to the top may be something that a lot of us are unwilling to do.

When people find themselves in a circumstance in which they feel an emotional need to succeed, they'll tend to find a way to do it. They didn't just try harder or rely on their natural intelligence or follow the advice of their forebears. They looked deep inside themselves to find any possible advantage they could and then used that advantage the best they could. The truth is that there are plenty of people with a lot of knowledge who aren't doing a whole lot with it. Then you've got a guy who knows only two things, but he uses what little he knows to consistently become ultrasuccessful. It's not necessarily about what you know or how smart you are; it's about your willingness to use the resources around you, take a look at who you are, and use everything you've got. *Everything.*

Many of us don't want to admit that we need something besides hard work and skill. We're not willing to look around us at the choices, circumstances, situations, and people that are holding us back. We're not willing to take risks at the moment when a risk would move us forward. We're not willing to listen and learn from people who are already successful. We just believe it should be done like all those other books and videos and experts and parents tell us: If you want success badly enough, you can achieve it.

In some sense, that's true. You do need to want to do the things I've laid out in this book. But successful people know that wanting success and needing it are two different things. I think the people who are ultimately successful really need that success—without it, they feel almost incomplete. That urge creates a natural drive to succeed. In that transition from want to need, a lot of things happen. If I want a drink of water but I'm kind of busy, I can wait. But when I *need* a drink of water—if I'm in the desert about to die—I *need* a drink of water. I'll do *whatever* it takes to get that drink of water. The bottom line is that you need to do what it takes to move your life forward—sometimes things you'd never anticipate doing. I don't mean breaking the law or harming others, as I've stated several times in this book. I'm talking about getting past what is holding you back, even if it's the very thing that got you where you are now.

And of course having something and using it aren't the same thing at all. The most successful people weren't necessarily multi-talented; they just used whatever they had. A lot of people have great gifts and talents and abilities and advantages, and they don't use them. Others have very few talents but make the most of what they have. I've got only about two or three usable talents, but I use them all the time.

You also need to be able to recognize the situations in which your personal advantage just will not work. You need to be able to say, "Hey, maybe I don't have the talent. Who knew I sucked this bad? I didn't know. I went out and I gave it my best shot. And I did it." One time I went to a talent contest and saw a guy singing, terribly—not as a joke; he really thought he could sing. I looked in his eyes and witnessed the exact moment he realized he couldn't. His face said, "Wait a minute. I'm hitting a high note, and everybody's looking at me with a weird look on their face." So he started looking back at the audience with a weird look on his face. The awkwardness was unbelievable. But his discomfort had an upside—he was given the opportunity to acknowledge that he lacked that talent. So then he could move on to something he might actually be good at. Something that would not involve any sounds he might make. I don't know what this guy's doing now, but I'm sure it's not singing. Which is *really* good for everybody.

Are you willing to take that honest look at yourself? You've reached the point where you need to do this on your own with this book as your guide. People like Armando, the wholesaler in Chapter 7, can inspire you. The next chapter can serve as one final reminder of what you've read as you start to create your personal advantages. But only you can look at yourself deeply and do what it takes to reach higher. Start by taking a look at some of the lies you believe. Ask yourself the question: Is there something that I believe that might not be true? Ask those questions about yourself and others.

We are all capable of succeeding if we remember one thing before we even start: Business, like life, is not a fair fight. You're going to come across people who've found better opportunities or are in better situations than you, so you need every advantage you can get.

The top 1 percent know how to set themselves up with those advantages that allowed them to win consistently. They weren't winning all the time because they battled it out to the end, fought to the death, and barely made it. They won by a lot. It was a lopsided victory. Every unfair fight is. Why would I want to be in a fair fight? Personally, I like to have every advantage I can, and so should you. Anyone can lose a fair fight! The goal is to consistently put ourselves in fights we can actually win. That's the truth about success. It's more than just leveling the playing field; it's using what you have to tilt the scales decidedly in your favor.

10

———

For the Lazy Reader

———

Quick advice for people who'll pretend they've read the book

OKAY, YOU JUST BOUGHT THIS BOOK AND HAVE MADE A SHOCKING discovery: You don't read! It's not that you can't read; you just don't have time, you're too impatient, you have a lot of e-mail to go through, or you simply have trouble focusing on anything that you can't get instant gratification from or eat!

This is not a problem, and don't feel devalued. If it were not for people who don't want to read, not much would be accomplished in the world. The superbusy, ADD, manic go-getters are the backbone of the business world. If everyone curled up with a good book, the world would come to a screeching halt, not to mention how nerdy it would look. The world needs readers, it's true, but we need you as well. Welcome, nonnerdy nonreading radicals. Your chapter awaits.

If you've made it through the book, this chapter serves as a quick recap of what we covered. If you haven't had the chance to get to all (or any) of the chapters and need to pretend to have read this book to look good in front of your boss or peers, this final chapter gives you the basics of what you need to know. And if you are too lazy to read even this, just look at the quotes in the headings, and you can at least sound like you know what other people are talking about. And if you don't have time to read the quotes, have your kids do it for you. You'll need them to be successful when you're not.

"Most successful businesspeople get where they are because they have a secret advantage, and they're not afraid to use it."

Our research showed that top performers in every industry are carefully guarding the real truth of their success—that some secret personal advantage catapulted them to the top. They used a personal advantage to position them as a trustworthy, easily understood solution. Whether they sought a job or influence, they made sure that everything they did looked like the solution. They had people believing in what they did before they did it. They had *instant image impact*. Competitors might call their secret advantage an unfair advantage, but it's exactly what we all want in our corner to stage an unfair fight. Because really, the fair fight is overrated. I can lose a fair fight! Give me an unfair fight *and* the upper hand—I'll take those odds any day.

"All I ever wanted in life was an unfair advantage."

The unfair fight is not a dirty fight; it's just an unfair one in which the opponents are not equally matched. The top performers we profile did nothing underhanded to get the upper hand. It's just that some had a way of doing things that positioned them so well from the start that they got not only better results but better *perceived* results thanks to their advantage.

"Remember, if you think your boss is stupid, that person is just smart enough to be your boss. The smartest people in the world are not in charge; they work for the action takers."

The reason the top 1 percent will not tell you how they became so successful is that the truth often does not sound impressive enough. They put the odds in their favor by being clear and direct and knowing what people need in order to feel satisfied and important. Their success was about whom they knew and how they reacted—not about superior ideas, genius, and sheer force of will! The *real* truth about success is that it's a bit too real. Sometimes our greatness is just not cool enough to brag about! If people knew how hard one task was for you and how easy another one was, they might think you're just kind of a lucky loser. In the worst-case scenario, some people are so hopelessly pathetic that they naturally attract a lot of support. As a result, they have help they would never receive if they were somewhat *less* pathetic. That's proof that some advantages should definitely be kept secret!

"Approach life talent first. Find or create your personal advantage."

You might not have innate advantages. Maybe you are short, or lack wow-'em smarts or cleverness. I know what you're thinking—"Just shoot me!" Hold up, negative Nancy. The truth is that you can create your own advantage. The top 1 percent of industry leaders we interviewed have discovered innate secret advantages and created new ones; you can too. Take a look at the advantages others have exploited and use them as a launching pad to identify your own innate advantage. Make the effort. After you determine what you bring to the table, you can start to level the playing field (or even make it really lopsided) by creating your own advantage like a lot of people we've covered in this book. What is your unique, distinctive edge? It might be your look, your personality, a character trait, your demeanor, the people you know, the resources you possess, or even a well-crafted plan to bolster your popularity in the workplace. You might be so lazy that you know the easiest way to be successful. Whatever it may be, everyone has an untapped advantage. Finding that edge and using it effectively is what separates the top 1 percent from the remaining 99 percent.

"Satisfaction may be the goal of the average person, but it is the enemy of greatness."

No offense (which is what people say right before they offend you), but sometimes a skill set isn't your trump card. Maybe it's the people around you. Are you willing to leverage the relationships you have? Are you really willing to build on the relationships with people you already know to get to the people you really need to know? Some might think that this is a manipulative approach, and that's when you have to ask yourself whether you are willing to ditch the loser buddies and the horse you rode in on and do what it takes to be successful. Leverage the resources and relationships around you that will contribute to your success. Take a look at what's working, and be honest about what isn't. If you are not satisfied with the results of your efforts, it's okay. One of the common traits of the top 1 percent is that their lack of satisfaction propels them forward. I take a look at myself all the time to see how I'm viewed. If my advantage is not working, I either alter my approach to the best of my abilities or, as I did in most cases, find a way to make my problems work for me! In the words of Spider-Man, "My gift is my curse."

"Long-term success is the result of relationships built on a foundation of trust. People get more value from those they trust."

The truth about success—being the best versus being consistently chosen as the best—is that a lot of people are good at what they do and have talent. But to be consistently chosen, there are specific things you need to do, and some tried-and-true methods still hold water. Take a look at those ages-old axioms about success. Then take a deep look at yourself and see if you're on track. Are you even in the ballpark? Have you even seen a ballpark? Some of the people we interviewed hadn't done anything tremendously groundbreaking, but they were successful anyway. In many cases, their simple answers didn't reveal enough to establish them as number one in their company, industry, or profession. This left us asking, "Surely there's something else?" But they all had achieved a degree of trust, clarity, and comfort with the people they worked with and had built that trust on a foundation of two things: compassion and competence.

"It does not matter how smart you are if nobody knows what you are talking about."

The common answers top performers gave about the reasons for their success also revealed that the top 1 percent often did something different, something most people deem irrelevant—they listened for things they could agree with, and they kept their processes or solutions simple. They made people comfortable with what they had to offer, which reinforced their value. The top 1 percent know that being the best is irrelevant. It's all fine and dandy if your product, idea, or solution is the best, but you hedge your bets for success if you are clear and likable and make people feel comfortable and important. I'm not saying that skill and good ideas are not valuable; I'm just saying our research showed that they are not what the most successful people had in common.

"Knowledge is not power; implementation is power."

Willingness to use an advantage is just as important as discovering it. Cross that line from knowledge to implementation, and be willing to act! Not everybody is. Many need to be coaxed into utilizing their distinctive edge to their advantage. Most people tend to draw a line in the sand or create a boundary they're unwilling (or afraid) to cross. Many of these are not based on ethical or legal bounds; they're rooted in personal fears of how others will perceive us. Can you step back and look beyond the conventional business culture? Are you willing to take a chance? Can you create a plan for yourself? Can you adapt your beliefs in order to utilize your advantage?

Creating that willingness to actually *utilize* your edge is how you achieve greater success. The funny thing about willingness is that it's like opening a door. If you just crack it a little, you'll find it's relatively easy to move forward from there. But you first have to turn the knob and push. If you start with a little willingness to change or improve in certain areas, you'll soon find it easier to tackle other areas of your life or business relationships. But if you aren't willing to look at all or if you try to avoid delving into some particular area, you'll wind up stalled. Any advantage that gets you noticed is worth pursuing. Opening a door just a little bit is much easier than worrying about all the closed doors in life you'll have to go through to become successful. Knowing something and doing it have very little in common!

"Action and flexibility create opportunity."

Discovering and being willing to use your edge will only prepare you for battle. Your next move involves some strategic planning and flexible decision making about when and how to deploy this personal advantage to best effect. Just because you're a competent driver at speeds of 200 miles per hour doesn't mean you should exercise that particular skill daily on America's highways. Habitually drive like mad on a NASCAR track? Win titles, trophies, esteem, and prize money. Habitually drive like mad on Interstate 95? Win a trip to jail and lose your license (not to mention how the police feel about your roadside champagne celebration). The advantage really plays like an advantage only when it's used in a particular environment or arena.

Once you happen upon something that yields results, you need to build it into the culture of what you're doing and create a repeatable process that you can responsibly ride to success. You also need to be flexible enough to employ your advantage in situations where it makes the most sense to you. Now you're taking action, you're adapting along the way, and you're creating opportunity. Action and flexibility allow me to choose the opportunity that's right for me. It also gives me the power to decide what I don't want as well. So now I only draw lines in the sand based on the value system that I choose. For example, I don't eat Spam because of that gelatin goop that's used to slide it into the can. I refuse to eat any food that comes with its own lubricant! Spam is a fine product, I'm sure, and loved by many—just not by me. We don't have to live by the value systems of others and try to follow a path that does not fit who we are. It's time to capitalize on the opportunities that your advantages create.

"Circumstances do not create the quality of your life."

So, what are you waiting for? You have made it to the end of this chapter, proving your laziness is not an obstacle. Get out there and find your personal advantage and use it to succeed. It's you, only better. It's not unethical or wrong to use every resource you can get your hands on, as long as you are not hurting others. That's how all civilizations were built. They looked at what they had to work with and did the best they could. But it's important to note that not everyone was able to be successful, just the people willing to use the resources. Life is not fair; some people are dealt negative circumstances and have to find a way past them in order to succeed. It's like superstitions. There was no justice in the Salem witch trials; you could be convicted for showing up in another person's dreams. (If you think our court system is strange now, look where it came from: "Your honor, thee approached me in a devilish manner as I dreamt!") But once we got past the evil dreamers and scarlet letters, we progressed. There is an old saying, "You have to play the cards you're dealt." What if your cards suck? What if the cards you hold could never get you where you want to go? That's it? I'm done? I'm born mediocre and game over? Circumstances do not create the quality of your life—you create the quality of your life. It's called *your life* because you get to decide how it feels to live it.

Index

About the Author

Garrison Wynn is a former professional stand-up comedian and the founder of Wynn Solutions, a firm that provides business strategies and influence techniques to audiences around the world. In his teens, Wynn worked with Magnavox and Hank Aaron to promote the world's first video gaming system, and by age 27, he became the youngest department head in a Fortune 500 company's history. He lives in Houston, Texas.